DEVELOPING
Mindful Students, Skillful Thinkers, Thoughtful Schools

DEVELOPING
Mindful Students, Skillful Thinkers, Thoughtful Schools

Martin Buoncristiani
Patricia Buoncristiani
Foreword by Arthur L. Costa

CORWIN
A SAGE Company

CORWIN
A SAGE Company

FOR INFORMATION:

Corwin
A SAGE Company
2455 Teller Road
Thousand Oaks, California 91320
(800) 233-9936
www.corwin.com

SAGE Publications Ltd.
1 Oliver's Yard
55 City Road
London EC1Y 1SP
United Kingdom

SAGE Publications India Pvt. Ltd.
B 1/I 1 Mohan Cooperative Industrial Area
Mathura Road, New Delhi 110 044
India

SAGE Publications Asia-Pacific Pte. Ltd.
3 Church Street
#10-04 Samsung Hub
Singapore 049483

Acquisitions Editor: Debra Stollenwerk
Associated Editor: Desirée A. Bartlett
Editorial Assistant: Kimberly Greenberg
Production Editor: Cassandra Margaret Seibel
Copy Editor: Alan Cook
Typesetter: C&M Digitals (P) Ltd.
Proofreader: Rae-Ann Goodwin
Indexer: Terri Corry
Cover Designer: Scott Van Atta
Permissions Editor: Adele Hutchinson

Copyright © 2012 by Corwin

Printed in the United States of America

Library of Congress Cataloging-in-Publication Data

Buoncristiani, Martin.

Developing mindful students, skillful thinkers, thoughtful schools / Martin and Patricia Buoncristiani.

p. cm.
Includes bibliographical references and index.

ISBN 978-1-4522-2014-7 (pbk.)

1. Thought and thinking—Study and teaching.
2. Metacognition in children. 3. School improvement programs. I. Buoncristiani, Patricia. II. Title.

LB1590.3.B86 2012
370.15′2—dc23   2011036716

This book is printed on acid-free paper

MIX
Paper from
responsible sources
FSC® C014174
www.fsc.org

12 13 14 15 16 10 9 8 7 6 5 4 3 2 1

Contents

Foreword

Drawing on our knowledge of the forces of nature, we know that opposites attract. And that's one reason why this book is so attractive. The authors originate from opposite hemispheres. Martin is from North America, while Pat is from Australia. Thus, their view of education, thinking, and learning reflects a global perspective. But hemisphericity doesn't stop there.

The two hemispheres of the brain have different functions. The left side of the brain is the logical hemisphere; it is analytical, rational, and is particularly involved in language. Martin's background experience is in science and engineering—logical, sequential, and mathematical.

The right side of the brain is the creative and intuitive hemisphere, gathering information from images and interpreting patterns and body language, emotional content, and tone of voice. Pat's background is education and literacy—relational, creative, and intuitive.

People often describe themselves as either left-brained or right-brained, but in reality we all use both sides of our brains, and we learn best when both sides work together to analyze and synthesize experiences and information. And that is another reason why this book is so powerful. Both authors work together to help us understand effective, critical, creative, skillful thinking; to make application to schools, classrooms, and learners; and to build more thoughtful world futures.

Their mutually supportive views and vast experiences weave together the neuroscientific research about the ways the brain develops over time and operates when solving problems. They offer numerous educational applications for teachers and curriculum workers to more expertly create classroom conditions, instructional strategies, and curriculum maps that liberate learners' creative potentials, enhance rational decision making, and develop their propensity for continuous lifelong learning.

At the center of their message is the plea to focus energies on the development of that uniquely human capacity, metacognition—being aware of, monitoring, and evaluating one's own thinking. They, along with numerous neuroscientists and cognitive psychologists, believe that humans possess the potential for becoming more "mindful" about the self-regulation of their minds.

These thinking skills and Habits of Mind are not just "kid stuff." The capacity for greater mindfulness extends to adults as continuous learners as well as to students who are in the process of becoming continuous learners. Effective, conscious teachers monitor themselves, their intentions, their questions, their nonjudgmental response behaviors, and the effects that are produced in their students. Teachers are deliberate in their planning and in their application and tracking of diverse instructional strategies that fit the unique styles and developmental levels of their students.

With proper instruction, students too can learn to control and direct these executive processes. Thus, the thinking skills and Habits of Mind described in this book may serve as an internal compass that mindful humans employ when confronted with problematic situations by asking themselves, "What is the most *intelligent thing* I can do right now?"

- How might I learn from this? What are my resources? How can I draw on my past successes with problems like this? What do I already know about the problem? What resources do I have available or need to generate?
- How might I approach this problem *flexibly?* How might I look at the situation in another way? How can I draw upon my repertoire of problem-solving strategies? How can I look at this problem from a fresh perspective (*lateral thinking*)?
- How might I illuminate this problem to make it clearer or more precise? Do I need to check out my data sources? How might I break this problem down into its component parts and develop a strategy for understanding and accomplishing each step?
- What do I know or not know? What questions do I need to ask? What strategies are in my mind now? What am I aware of in terms of my own beliefs, values, and goals with this problem? What feelings or emotions am I aware of that might be blocking or enhancing my progress?
- The interdependent thinker might turn to others for help. He or she might ask: How does this problem affect others? How can we solve it together, and what can I learn from others that would help me become a better problem solver?

Taking a reflective stance in the midst of active problem solving is often difficult. There is no such thing as perfect mindfulness. It is an ideal state toward which we constantly aspire. While every human is capable of generating self-reflective consciousness, not everyone seems to use it equally. The intent of this book is to provide strategies, tools, and resources for parents, teachers, and organizational leaders to enhance those conditions that will continually grow and develop these cognitive capacities in all individuals in the organization.

Educators today are being admonished and even coerced to abide by state and federal mandates to teach toward achievement tests, to follow scripted lessons, to categorize and label students, and to succumb to teacher evaluation and "politically correct" laws and policies that demean students and demoralize teachers. The authors' goal for education, therefore, is to support teachers and students in liberating, developing, and habituating these human intellectual capacities more fully. Taken together, these capacities are a force directing us toward increasingly authentic, congruent, and ethical behavior, the touchstones of integrity. They are the tools of disciplined choice making. They are the primary vehicles in the lifelong journey toward integration. They are the "right stuff" that makes human beings efficacious.

The authors are among a growing alliance of global mind workers who are endeavoring to make the world a more compassionate, cooperative, and thought-full place. This book provides a compelling invitation to join this crusade.

Arthur L. Costa, EdD
Professor Emeritus
California State University, Sacramento

Preface

To Become a Nation of Skillful Thinkers

We, as teachers, find ourselves facing a continual reinvention of our educational systems. But revised curricula, new testing mandates, increased levels of accountability, and rapidly evolving educational technology don't seem to be pulling us out of the malaise that bedevils us at the speed that the world demands. Perhaps we have been looking in the wrong places.

In this book we offer a unique perspective on the teaching of thinking because

1. The ability to think metacognitively is essential if we expect our students to be prepared to live productively in a rapidly changing world. This book focuses on the teaching of metacognition to children so they will become more skillful thinkers and independent, lifelong learners.

2. This book provides an easy access to the theories underlying classroom practices. Teachers who read this book will understand why they do what they do.

3. This book demonstrates practical ways in which school and home can cooperate to create vibrant learning communities.

Our Rationale for Writing This Book

The United States of America has forged a powerful presence in the world based primarily on the strength of our economy. Our economic growth over the last century was due predominantly to developing new technologies. "Economic studies conducted even before the information-technology revolution have shown that as much as 85% of measured growth in U.S. income per capita was due to technological change" (National Research Council, 2006, p. 1). Our continued success in an increasingly global economy must be built on the foundation of a skilled and innovative *next generation.* There is growing evidence that we may not be producing that generation with our current educational practices.

An awareness that something is seriously amiss in education in the United States prompted legislators to ask the National Academy of Science to review the current condition of U.S. science education and to recommend the top 10 actions that Congress might take to insure that we remain leaders in innovation. The preamble to the ensuing report *Rising Above the Gathering Storm* (National Research Council, 2006) states, "Having reviewed trends in the United States and abroad, the committee is deeply concerned that the scientific and technological building blocks critical to our economic leadership are eroding at a time when many other nations are gathering strength" (p. 3). Norman Augustine, chairman of the committee producing this report, stated further that America today faces a serious and intensifying challenge with regard to its future competitiveness and standard of living and that we appear to be on a losing path.

Thomson Reuters Research Analytics tracks trends and performance in basic research. It has compiled comparative data from 1981 to 2009 measuring the production of research papers in science, engineering, and materials science from countries throughout the world. This information was released in two reports appearing in 2005 and 2010 (Adams & Pendlebury, 2010; "U. S. slide in world share continues," 2005). The first of these reports, from the online magazine *Science Watch,* shows

1. a steady decline in the U.S. contribution to world science,

2. a steady increase in the contribution from Asia Pacific countries, and

3. a relatively constant contribution from EU countries.

The 2010 report shows that

the 20th century was largely dominated by the U.S. as a major powerhouse of scientific research and innovation, with 40% of the papers indexed in the *Web of Science* fielded by U.S.

scientists in the 1990s. By 2009, that figure was down to 29%. The U.S. now struggles to keep pace with increased output from Europe and Asia. Yet research impact and the overall reputation of higher education institutions in the U.S. remain strong. (Thomson Reuters, n.d.)

This trend is mirrored in the growing production of PhDs in science, mathematics, and technology in China compared to the declining numbers in the United States. Our nation faces a future in which it is no longer dominant in the fields of science, mathematics, and engineering.

Further, evidence of the unsatisfactory academic performance of U.S. students comes from a major international study of student progress, the Program for International Student Assessment (PISA). This test, developed by the Organisation for Economic Co-operation and Development, examines students from the major developed countries—countries responsible for roughly 90% of the world economy. PISA tests 15-year-olds in mathematics, science, and reading every three years. The United States consistently performs at or below the average in each of these three subject areas, despite the fact that we spend more per capita on education than almost every other developed nation.

The United States performs a bit better on another test, the Trends in International Mathematics and Science Study (TIMSS), which tests students in grades 4 and 8 every four years. However, the cultural diversity in TIMMS is very wide, including countries like Botswana, Mongolia, Denmark, Australia, Palestine, England, and Canada. In addition, the focus of the two tests are significantly different; PISA measures the *ability of students to apply their knowledge and skills to meet real-life challenges,* whereas TIMMS measures the extent to which students have *mastered the taught curriculum* (Gonzales et al., 2004; Programme for International Student Assessment, 2003).

Our survival as a major economic and political power in the world is at risk if we cannot maintain our global competitiveness with a well-educated next generation. It simply isn't good enough that, when our 15-year-olds are asked to apply their learning, they perform at or below average compared with the rest of the developed world.

That is the bad news; now here is the good news. At a time when we face this growing global challenge from the developing world, our emerging understanding of the human brain provides a means to rise to this challenge. Research from a variety of disciplines has produced a new picture of how the brain operates and how it learns most effectively, a picture that emphasizes the brain's *plasticity*—it is an organ capable of continuous improvement and change. This new knowledge not only helps to explain how the brain operates, it also provides a means of self-understanding that can lead to new ways of learning—the skill of metacognition. Educational practices need to move beyond endless reforms of curriculum and assessment and accountability measures and incorporate these new understandings into the ways in which we do things in our schools and colleges.

The Focus of the Book Is on Thinking About Thinking

So this is a book about *metacognition,* a long word which means thinking about how we think. It is an important concept because it is only by thinking about how we think that we can consciously and continuously improve our thinking. It is the only way to become skillful thinkers and independent learners.

The book is directed to teachers and school administrators who want to see their students transformed into skillful thinkers and their schools transformed into thoughtful and thought-filled places of learning. Skillful thinkers can adapt their thinking to new situations and transform what they learn in one context into another. When faced with new problems, they can formulate a plan of action and proceed to a solution. In a society where readiness for work is an increasingly significant factor in educational planning, we need to remain alert to the fact that if we train a young person with the skills required for a particular job and that job disappears, then he is trained for something that no longer exists. But if we educate young people who are flexible, metacognitive thinkers, they will be able to adapt their learning and find their way successfully in new territory.

Chapter 1 discusses the two major forces acting to change traditional education: first, the knowledge that the brain is plastic, which implies that we need to teach students how to use this flexibility, and how to think about their thinking so they can control their learning; and second, the global revolution in information and communication technology, which is changing the way people work, which in turn mandates a change in how students are prepared in order to deal with this changing workplace. In fact, many of the jobs that students entering school for the first time this year will be expected to fill a decade and a half later are not even defined yet.

Chapter 2 summarizes the relevant brain research on how people learn and introduces the principles of metacognition that underlie this work. We provide sufficient depth to justify the techniques for enhanced learning that follow and point readers to additional resources, should they wish to delve deeper.

Chapters 3, 4, 5, and 6 deal directly with metacognition, defining it carefully, deconstructing it into its constituents, and finally discussing the importance of language to metacognition. Chapters 7 and 8 focus on the implementation of metacognition, first in problem solving and then in the organization of knowledge. The final three chapters, 9, 10, and 11, provide strategies and tools for teaching thinking. Chapter 9 looks particularly at the role of questioning in eliciting metacognition and deeper levels of thinking. Chapter 10 provides some very practical strategies both for metacognitive note taking and for assessment that recognize the significance of metacognition, and in Chapter 11 we examine what schools can do to create a culture of metacognitive thinking throughout the school and in partnerships in learning with parents.

The final section provides a set of practical resources for teachers to help encourage metacognition with their students. It also provides materials schools can use to encourage and inform parents of ways they can participate in their children's learning.

A Personal Perspective on How We Came to Write This Book

In a time when lives are lived at a fast pace and dinner-table conversation has become a rarity in many households, we have stuck to the old traditions and share our thoughts about events of the day around the dinner table in the evening. It was these conversations that provided the genesis of this book. We often began discussions that grew out of our own frustrations as educators.

Pat was an elementary school principal in the United States. She would describe the difficulties of trying to create a productive learning environment in a low-achieving and disadvantaged school. The problems seemed to come from every level: difficulties with parents, with students, with teachers, and with administrators.

At the same time Martin, a university professor of physics, was struggling to help his students achieve a conceptual understanding of science. While these students learned facts and simple procedures easily, when faced with questions or problems that required a deeper understanding of the concepts involved, they faltered. As these discussions progressed, it became clear to us that the problems of these two different pedagogical situations had similar roots. Both had to do with thinking.

In a system relentlessly focused on standardized test results, school accreditation, and data analysis, Pat was fearful that there was so much focus on the development of test-taking skills, the memorization of content, and the learning of routines and formulaic responses to test questions that the teaching of skillful thinking and understanding was taking a back seat. Awakening in students an understanding of their own thinking processes and teaching them how to think skillfully is a complex, time-consuming process. There never seemed to be time for this as pressures increased to cover curriculum content before the next round of testing.

When the school district brought Dr. Arthur Costa to provide professional development to principals, it was an "Aha!" moment. Costa introduced a list of habits or dispositions that characterize the behavior of successful people facing complex problems. He called this list the *Habits of Mind*. It became crystal clear that the path to lifelong, independent learning had to include the teaching of thinking. It was not an optional extra, but was fundamental to the success of every other kind of learning. Without the teaching of thinking, all of the test taking and passing in the world would not develop lifelong learning skills. It also became clear that this was not just something that applied only to schoolchildren.

All the adults involved in the endeavor—the parents, the teachers and the administrators—needed to be skilled thinkers as well. Skilled thinking needed to be part of the world outside the classroom—in government, in civic responsibility and participation, and in the workplace. The Habits of Mind provide a structure within which educators, parents, and the wider community can organize all the things we know to be so important about learning but have been in danger of forgetting. It also finally gives us a straightforward, jargon-free language that will enable us to talk about our thinking.

Over the last 20 years, Martin's primary concern in teaching physics at the university level had been to have students come to understand underlying concepts. It was not too difficult to teach students to solve simple physics problems expressed verbally, to plug in the numbers and turn the mathematical crank. But when students were asked questions that involved a deeper understanding of underlying concepts, they often became confused about what was being asked. They seemed to have no clear thinking procedures they could apply to sort out their confusion. For example, in learning about motion, students learn about how objects move under the influence of gravity near the surface of the earth—about the flight of soccer balls and such. At another point they also learn about the forces required to keep an object moving in a circle. They are able to understand each of these two concepts individually. However, when faced with a question like "Why does an object dropped near the surface of the earth fall while the same object dropped in a space capsule floats?" many students respond by stating that gravity at the space capsule is much weaker than on earth. In fact, the gravitational force is only about 5% less in a low-earth orbit. Students found it difficult to combine their understanding of gravity and circular motion to answer the question; moreover, they often didn't know what steps to take to resolve the question.

Martin tried to engage the students in classroom discussions about how they were thinking, but it became clear that the content language, the language of physics and mathematics, was not sufficient to address all aspects of the students' thinking. Something else was needed. When Pat told him about Art Costa's visit to her school district and the Habits of Mind, he too saw the light. Together they began a systematic exploration of what else in addition to content is needed to engage students in a discussion about their own thinking and learning and, in the process, deepen conceptual learning. The result of that exploration is this book.

We were most influenced by three specific pieces of work: the National Research Council reports on *How People Learn*, the circle of ideas surrounding the Habits of Mind of Costa and Kallick, and the metastudies by the Mid-Continent Regional Education Laboratory and Robert Marzano describing effective teaching and learning strategies.

The *How People Learn* series explores the research of a broad range of experts in most aspects of learning (National Research Council, 1999, 2000, 2005). Its findings clarify the three most fundamental aspects of flexible learning:

- understanding and dealing with prior knowledge of a subject;
- understanding how knowledge is organized in one's brain; and
- the importance of thinking about one's own thinking, or meta-cognition.

The work of Costa and Kallick builds on this framework by providing and elaborating on a set of dispositions or habits that characterize successful people (Costa & Kallick, 2000, 2008). These are the habits used by skillful thinkers who know how to behave when faced with complex problems and who are flexible learners.

Robert Marzano has identified a set of strategies that are used by successful teachers (Marzano, Pickering, & Pollock, 2001). We demonstrate in this book how many of these strategies can be used by teachers from pre-primary to tertiary levels as they develop learners with the ability to think effectively and become independent, lifelong learners.

The more completely we understand the thinking processes involved in learning and problem solving, the more likely we are to be able to monitor and adjust our practices in ways that further successful behaviors. We are not advocating endless navel-gazing and introspection. When confronted with problems, we need to find solutions and act on them in a timely fashion. But shooting from the hip has gotten us into a great deal of trouble, personally, socially, and politically. As we face the increasingly complex problems in our schools, our homes, and in the workplaces of our nation, we need to understand what we are doing, we need to think before we act, and we need to be sure that our thinking is explicit and appropriate. It is imperative that we think about our thinking!

We are grateful to many people: to Arthur Costa, who has been our constant source of encouragement and whose work with Bena Kallick was our inspiration at the start of our journey; to James Anderson and Elaine Brownlow, who supported our efforts in Australia; to Raj Chaudhury and Randy Caton in the United States for many useful discussions; to Richard Bartley, who was for Pat an important mentor; and to Deborah Stollenwerk and Alan Cook, who have guided us gently through the intricacies of editing.

We dedicate this book to the many classroom teachers in both the United States and Australia who have embraced these ideas and enriched our understanding as they shared their experiences and their thoughts.

Acknowledgments

Corwin would like to thank the following individuals for taking the time to provide their editorial insight:

Elizabeth Alvarez, Principal, John C. Dore Elementary School, Chicago, IL

Lynn Macan, Superintendent, Cobleskill-Richmondville Central School District, Cobleskill, NY

Tanna H. Nicely, Assistant Principal, Dogwood Elementary School, Knoxville, TN

Susan Stewart, Assistant Professor, Ashland University, Ashland, OH

Claudia J. Thompson, Academic Officer, Learning and Teaching Peninsula School District, Gig Harbor, WA

About the Authors

 **Martin Buoncristiani** is an emeritus professor of physics at Christopher Newport University in the United States. He has been dedicated to science and mathematics education for over 35 years. In his involvement in curricular development for the university, he has been a strong advocate of adapting teaching methods to our current understanding of how people learn. His scientific research has focused on lasers and optical science, and he was awarded the NASA Public Service Medal for his work developing instruments for atmospheric study. Throughout his career he has addressed K-12 science education, beginning with promotion of computers in the classroom in the 1970s and extending to the introduction of critical thinking skills in the current decade.

 **Patricia Buoncristiani** has spent over 30 years as an educator committed to the belief that learning how to think is the foundation for every successful learner. She has been a classroom teacher, a teachers college lecturer, and, most recently, a school principal in both Australia and the United States. Her experience includes work with school systems in the United Kingdom, the United States, and Australia. She has had extensive experience training educators in early literacy development, behavior management, and the development of thinking-based curricula.

Martin and Pat are cofounders of Thinking and Learning in Concert, an educational consultancy dedicated to integrating thinking and learning. Together they provide engaging, interactive, and dynamic workshops and presentations tailored to meet the specific needs of the group.

They can be contacted at ausatlc@aol.com and
http://thinkingandlearninginconcert.org/

1

Some Game Changers

The Brain, Intelligence, and the Role of Metacognition

In a time of drastic change it is the learners who inherit the future. The learned usually find themselves equipped to live in a world that no longer exists.

—Eric Hoffer (2006)

We now face a widely acknowledged need for significant changes in education. Almost every educational system in every developed country is going through some sort of process of evaluation and reformation. There are two primary reasons for this need to change our educational culture. The first is that the world around us is rapidly changing, with globalization and evolving telecommunications technology creating more and more competition for our industry (Friedman, 2005). To maintain our position in this globalized world (and to continue to support the development of emerging nations), we must remain the technological innovators we were in the last century. To do this, we must have a steady supply of talented young people interested in careers supporting the business and technology of the future. This, in turn, requires an education system that produces students who can think and learn.

The second reason for a change in education is that our view of the human brain and how it functions has led to a new view of human intelligence (National Research Council, 2000). With the change in our understanding of how people learn comes a revision of the idea of intelligence. Perhaps the most revealing recent discovery about the brain is that it is not the immutable organ it was thought to be during the first three quarters of the 20th century.

The brain is changeable and trainable. It changes in two important ways—new brain cells and new synapses can be formed by using it thoughtfully, and its blood supply is strengthened through physical exercise. This ability of the brain to change its structure is often referred to as *plasticity*. Each human brain is plastic; it is in a constant process of reforming itself. As our educational practices come to accommodate this new understanding of the nature of the brain, we will increasingly avoid the unsuccessful practices of the past. By teaching our children how to think and how to understand their own thought processes, we place them in control of their learning from the inside out. The student comes to know how he learns best and is no longer simply at the mercy of an external force, the teacher, directing his learning on the basis of the teacher's best guess about how the student learns most effectively.

We have a long history of teachers making their best guesses about how students learn. There was a time when simple, single measures such as IQ tests and various attainment tests were used to predict the future academic success of children. Students were streamed at an early age into more or less academically complex programs based on those test results. The high-scoring individuals were groomed for university and the professions, while the lower-scoring ones were pointed toward trades or semiskilled careers.

We have many examples of individuals who did poorly at some early point in their educational lives using the standard testing and evaluation procedures but have achieved great things in their adult lives. In a BBC Newsround interview in 2004, Richard Branson described himself as being at the bottom of the class when he eventually left school at the age of 15. He has revealed that he suffers from dyslexia but actually finds this to be an advantage in his dealings with the business world. Because he understands how he thinks, and hence has insight into both his strengths and weaknesses, he is able to judge the language of advertising, for example, ensuring that if he can understand it, then so can anyone. He has learned how to turn an apparent deficit into a real asset. His personal history demonstrates the problems inherent in a system that does not explore deeply enough the varieties of types of learning and the flexibility and potential of the human mind.

How many students have reached the age of 15 without understanding how they think and learn, simply because this was never taught to them? These students submit to their teachers' best guesses about how they learn, rather than growing in their own understanding and independence as lifelong learners. Too often they leave our schools because our schools have given up on them. The school has provided a rigid, prescribed curriculum where attainment is relentlessly tested for *all* students in the same manner in order to ensure standardization and comparability for accountability measures.

Our schools need to give students the power to explore their unique ways of thinking and help them discover how to make links, how to integrate new learning with things already known, how to create complex and dynamic mental maps, and how to make connections between the emotional and visual areas of their brains. Brains are not standardized. The brain you had when you picked up this book is subtly different from the brain you have now.

It is essential to remain sensitive to the balance between teaching a body of knowledge and developing the skills and attitudes needed to use that knowledge effectively and creatively. Curricula must reflect the importance of developing the habits of skillful thinking, as must training programs designed to make our young people ready for work. If the focus of education is on the acquisition of factual knowledge rather than on the ability to organize and transform knowledge through the application of skillful thinking, we risk developing a generation of "learned" students whose knowledge is inert and may rapidly become irrelevant.

It is important for all involved—students, teachers, and parents—to be aware of these new viewpoints on intelligence because

1. individuals can improve their own processes of learning and thinking;

2. skillful thinking and learning make knowledge more useful and transportable; and

3. we can initiate a lifelong process of continual development of the brain.

The continued prosperity of our society depends on our ability to think creatively and flexibly. These understandings about learning need to underpin our endeavors in any context—the school, the workplace, and the community at large.

New standards of learning are being developed worldwide to accommodate globalization and the changing view of how people think and learn. Often these standards emphasize the vital role of thinking skills. For example, the International Baccalaureate (IB) curriculum has an underlying philosophy to promote the education of the whole person.

> The IB approach to knowledge and education may be defined as "liberal education for human rationality." The primary goal of this form of education is to develop critical thinkers since the moral, social and political issues of the world often engage emotions and passions as well as intellect. Rational thinking is considered necessary to understand the difference between understanding, belief, feeling and truth. Opening up and developing the mind is the key to developing the powers of intelligence and rational thought. (Sobulis, 2005, p. 2)

Implications of the New View of Intelligence

The model of education most current teachers were taught under was developed at the beginning of the 20th century and was intended to prepare workers for the Industrial Revolution. We now need to prepare people for the 21st century—for the Information Age. This is a time that values deep conceptual understanding and innovative thinking.

This older view of education is based on the idea of a fixed brain—the concept that an individual inherits a fixed level of intellect from the genetic disposition of his or her parents. Eric Jensen puts this idea decisively to rest:

> It turns out that the "fixed brain" theory is not just dead wrong, but—embarrassingly—it may be doing a great deal of harm. The human brain is so malleable that it can be fixed at artificially low levels by giving it a diet of status quo. (Jensen, 2006, p. x)

The fixed brain idea leads to the notion that each student is, in some sense, an empty vessel, to be filled with knowledge from various trusted sources, and thus suggests that teachers should encourage classrooms in which students are passive absorbers of information. A more constructivist view of education assumes the student will create meaning through active processes of engagement, questioning, and effective thinking. The teacher in this classroom is neither the source nor the viaduct for all information. The teacher is the facilitator, creating an environment within which students can engage with knowledge at a complex level, manipulating it, transferring it, and structuring a conceptual framework within which new information can be integrated.

This can make teaching a risky business, because it adds a level of unpredictability. Experienced teachers are aware that the taught curriculum does not always match the learned curriculum and may sometimes wonder if the students who wrote the essays being graded had actually been in the same classroom that the teacher had been working with all term.

Whether we are talking about the student in a classroom learning about physics, a worker in an industrial setting mastering a new process, or a child at home trying to come to an understanding about a family dispute, we are dealing with human beings learning new things. This book grows out of two fundamental ideas about learning, both well established by research and validated by practice in formal and informal learning environments.

The first is that *we learn best when we are actively engaged in the process of our own learning*. In emphasizing the importance of engagement in learning, we have in mind not only the experience of hands-on or inquiry-based activities, but more importantly the direct involvement of the learner in *thinking about his or her own thought processes*—that is, metacognition.[1] In order to discuss metacognition, it is necessary to have a language and a structure to describe the various facets of cognition. We will introduce the tools needed to understand and communicate about thinking.

The second fundamental idea is that *individuals are best equipped to approach problems of any sort when they embrace those habits of mind that foster skillful and innovative thinking*.[2] The ability to think skillfully and to reflect on one's thinking is not an innate human characteristic but rather a proficiency that needs to be taught explicitly. We will explore effective techniques for integrating the teaching of thinking into all educational activities, be they in the classroom, on the playground, at home, or in the workplace. In these days of standardized testing, it is worth noting that not only is learning to think skillfully an important life skill, it is a definite asset in taking forced-choice tests.

It is our intention here to encourage the understanding and implementation of these fundamental ideas across the educational enterprise by encouraging parents, school administrators, teachers, and students to actively think about how they think, teach, and learn and, in that process, to develop and use sound habits of mind.

This book is intended for all educators, administrators as well as teachers, because we believe that skillful thinking transcends the disciplines and classrooms. Lessons learned about how to think in Grade 2 need to be transferred to Grade 3; lessons about thinking in social studies need to be transferable to science. Skillful thinking should be central to every faculty meeting and to every meeting, formal or informal, with parents. In other words, skillful thinking needs to permeate every activity and relationship that is a part of the educational enterprise. It needs to be a part of the culture. A school is also a workplace and a place closely tied to the homes of the children within its walls. Each stakeholder, within the school and at home, will better contribute to the goals of education when skillful thinking underlies every practice.

An essential question for the reader to bear in mind is "What do you want your students to be able to do years after they leave your classroom, school, or home?" In asking this question at conferences and workshops, we find a remarkably consistent set of answers. The valued outcomes of education are the ability to get along with other people, to be self-sustaining, to solve problems, and to continue learning. All of these attributes rest on a foundation of thinking skills.

What we have learned about how people learn also extends well beyond the school environment. While our primary focus is upon the educational environment, it is worth mentioning that if a workplace is to be a dynamic, viable enterprise in a volatile and challenging environment, it is essential that participants at all levels be engaged and understand how learning best takes place. As we strive to make our students ready for work, we would be well advised to keep this in mind. The skills that served us well 10 years ago will no longer suffice. The workplaces that survive and prosper will be those in which skillful, metacognitive thinking underlies the way things are done. Similarly, democratic societies depend for their success on an informed population able to thoughtfully participate in civic processes. The blind acceptance of clichés and jingoistic phrases and the rapid spread of rumors and misinformation can only take place when people have not brought skillful thinking to bear on the things they hear and read.

Perhaps the most important notion to emerge from the shifting paradigm in education is one emphasized repeatedly by Art Costa: "If we treat students as intelligent people, they will become more intelligent people."

THINKING DEEPER: DISCUSSION QUESTIONS

1. During your career as an educator, what significant revisions of education have you seen? You might consider revisions of the curriculum, assessment procedures, and teaching strategies. How would you assess the success of each?

2. Do you know anyone from your own experience whose life path did not follow that which teachers might have reasonably expected? Did things turn out better or worse than expected?

3. What do you want your students to be able to do when they have finished their formal schooling? Identify the three most important goals, and consider where you find evidence of explicit teaching directed toward them in your curriculum.

Endnotes

1. The term *metacognition* is used in many different ways. We use it to mean an individual's conscious thinking about cognition in a constructive manner, that is, thinking about our thought processes with the intention of understanding and improving them.

2. The term *habits of mind* is used in many different contexts. We use it here in two ways. First, in a general sense, as those cognitive dispositions that enables skillful and innovative thinking and second, in reference to a specific body of knowledge developed by Arthur Costa and Bena Kallick.

2

How People Learn

Education is what you have left when you have forgotten everything you learned in school.

—Albert Einstein

We expect each newborn to come into the world with the ability to learn how to walk. We watch with delight but no great surprise as the toddler becomes more and more confident in negotiating the obstacles in the world and gradually becomes a stable and confident walker and runner. We send our children off to school knowing that they can walk, run, and play. We also know that some of our children do it better than others. With opportunity and careful teaching, some of our walkers and runners become hurdlers, dancers, and gymnasts, while others will spend all their lives holding the banisters when they climb down stairs and tripping over their own feet. Some of us become flexible, elegant, and accomplished movers.

Similarly, every newborn comes into the world with the ability to learn how to think. We have all met the adult intellectual gymnasts, and we have all met the prejudiced, narrow-minded stumblers. The difference lies in how they were taught to think.

It matters deeply, in both a personal and a social sense, how well we think. The problems of this world are complex, and their solutions need to be subtle. Those of us who stumble through our lives are destined to make bad decisions and choices, to misunderstand those around us, and to be limited in our flexibility and ability to adapt to the inevitable and accelerating change around us. Society needs creative, flexible thinkers who understand how to analyze a problem, who have a wide repertoire of approaches to problem solving, and who can see problems from varying viewpoints. Living is a constant process of problem solving—within the family, the job, in government, in our practical day-to-day lives, and in our spiritual and philosophical responses to life. It is essential that we provide opportunities for our children to become skilled, elegant thinkers.

Research carried out over the last few decades by neuroscientists, medical professionals, cognitive psychologists, and anthropologists has led to a new view of the brain and how it functions. This new insight on the brain was, in part, enabled by the development of a series of measurement devices that allow a nonintrusive probe of the brain while it is performing specific tasks. Recognizing that this information was vital to educators, the United States National Academy of Science and the National Academy of Engineering commissioned two committees (the Committee on Developments in the Science of Learning and the Committee on Learning Research and Educational Practice) to examine this research with a particular view to understanding its implications for classroom practice. Their findings were published in a series of reports (National Research Council, 1999, 2000, 2005) that focused on three findings that should underpin everything we do in our schools if we hope to develop thoughtful, flexible lifelong learners.

The first of these findings deals with the knowledge students bring with them to the classroom.

Finding 1

Students come to the classroom with *preconceptions* about how the world works.

If their initial understanding is not engaged, they may fail to grasp the new concepts and information that are taught, or they may learn them for the purpose of a test but revert to their preconceptions outside the classroom.

Many student preconceptions come from their own efforts to figure out how the world works as they experience it. Others come from the things they are taught by teachers, parents, and their friends. Preconceptions can be deep-seated. They may actually appear to partially explain the world and consequently are difficult to change. Sometimes the true facts can be counterintuitive. For example, it may seem obvious to a child that heavy objects fall more rapidly than light ones. After all, when you drop a piece of paper, it floats gently to the ground while a baseball, much heavier than the paper, falls much more quickly. The child with this preconception is in good company, because Aristotle shared this view. It took the careful experiments of Galileo and the theoretical prowess of Newton to sort out the truth: When frictional forces like air resistance are eliminated, objects fall to earth at the same rate regardless of their weight.

Children have many common misconceptions about science: for example, that the seasons are caused by the Earth being closer to the Sun in the summer than in the winter, or that objects float because they are lighter than water. In mathematics, they may believe that the area inside a fixed-length loop of string is always the same because the length of the string is always the same or that multiplication always makes numbers bigger. In language arts, they may believe that poems must rhyme; furthermore, children have difficulty understanding nonliteral or figurative uses of language such as metaphor and verbal irony. Some misconceptions are acquired from others, such as the belief that people use only 10% of their brains. Generally, children have only partial understanding of common but complex ideas like illness and death, money, and religion.

Good teachers have always sought to find out how much students know before embarking on a new topic. They know they don't have time to waste teaching things the students already know. This finding suggests we should also discover what they *think* they know. Sometimes we need to teach and sometimes we need to "unteach." Preconceptions, when they are misconceptions, can significantly interfere with true learning. They can also be very difficult to change. We are particularly fond of the things we have worked out for ourselves, and we seem to become fonder of them as we grow older and the quantity of self-created explanations increases. "I know what I think. Stop confusing me with facts." "I've always done it this way. I'm not going to change now." A child, taught about infectious diseases, may hold her breath when walking past someone who sneezed or coughed, or had a sore on their face, or walked with a limp, or just "looked odd." The child overapplied the theory of infection. Misconceptions can be very deeply seated. For the child, many ideas about how the world works come from parents. Questionable ideas are accepted without hesitation because in the eyes of the young child, parents are always right: The goblins under the bed go away when mommy turns the light on, thunder is the sound of clouds bumping together, and the next-door neighbors are poor because they don't want to work hard.

Everything we say and do in the classroom is filtered in the child's mind through the preconceptions that color his world. Unless we uncover and address these preconceptions, we can never be sure that the student heard what the teacher actually said and not simply what he expected the teacher to say. Preconceptions have the power to significantly interfere with learning. In subsequent chapters, we discuss ways of uncovering the extent of student's prior knowledge and how to counter misconceptions.

The second finding deals with how the knowledge we acquire is lodged in our brains.

Finding 2

To develop competence in an area of inquiry, students must

   a. have a deep foundation of factual knowledge;

   b. understand facts and ideas in a context of a conceptual framework; and

   c. organize knowledge in ways that facilitate retrieval and application.

Teachers know what it is for a student to have a sound foundation of factual knowledge of a topic. Unfortunately, because factual knowledge is easier to test than conceptual understanding, remembered information and routines have become increasingly the focus of education, especially in those systems in which high-stakes testing are a central feature of accountability. Understanding the conceptual framework and how knowledge is organized within the learner's mind is complex. We return to this subject and explore how knowledge is organized in our minds in Chapter 8.

At this point, it is useful to consider how you have organized one of your own areas of expertise with the following thinking exercise.

Thinking Exercise

Each of us has several areas of expertise. You may be an expert at teaching reading, baking bread, hang gliding, quilting, gardening, scuba diving, wine tasting, or something else.

1. Think of one area of your own personal expertise and list the types of *factual information and skills* you need to be an expert in that area. For example, if sailing is your area you need knowledge of weather, winds and currents, navigation, how to set sails, and similar matters.

2. Now examine your list of knowledge and skills and think of *how you organize it in your mind.* Can you make a map of how these pieces of knowledge are interconnected? Is there a particular sequence in which you call upon this knowledge?

To illustrate the importance of organizing knowledge as it is learned, we can think of two broad categories of learners: novices and experts. Novices treat each new bit of information as independent and unconnected, while experts recognize patterns of meaning and have developed a context for new information. For example, with regard to the knowledge to be acquired in the third grade, we can consider a child entering the classroom on the first day of the academic year as a novice and a student who has completed third grade successfully as an expert.

There has been significant research on the differences between novices and experts. A particularly clear example, reported in *How People Learn,* involved research carried out by de Groot (1965). This study tested the knowledge of chessboard patterns of three individuals: a chess master, a very good chess player, and a beginning player (novice). A chessboard was set up to represent a possible midgame pattern with 24 pieces on the board. Each individual was shown the setup for just one minute and asked to reproduce the pattern of pieces. When they had done this to the best of their ability, they were shown the original board again for another minute and asked to correct their first attempt. This was repeated several times and the results are shown in the graph in Figure 2.1.

After the first trial, the chess master had 16 of the 24 pieces correctly placed, whereas the good player had 8 correct, and the beginner only 4. The chess master got all pieces correctly placed after four trials and the good player took five. The beginner still had two pieces out of place after seven trials. Clearly, each player had knowledge of

Figure 2.1	This graph shows the results of de Groot's experiment on recognizing the placement of chess pieces by players of different levels of expertise.

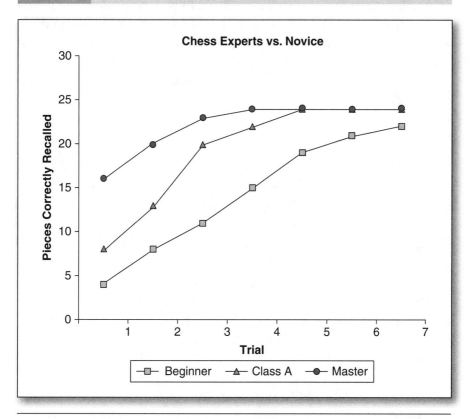

Source: This figure was obtained from *How People Learn* (National Research Council, 2000).

the game, but two players could easily transfer that knowledge to the situation posed in the experiment.

The knowledge of chess in the minds of the master and the good player was organized in such a way that they could recognize patterns and understand the sequences of moves that got their pieces to where they were on the board. For the novice without that well-organized structure, each chess piece was a discreet entity only superficially related to each other piece.

Experts acquire new information and organize it differently from novices. They organize information so that it can be transferred to different situations; that is, knowledge acquired in one context can be applied in other contexts. Experts are able to recognize patterns and to understand sequences and logical or temporal connections between discrete items of information.

An expert—for example a teacher—may transfer (teach) information they possess, but they cannot transfer their own personal context or organization of that information. The organization of knowledge takes place in the student's own mind. To become expert, a student should think about how he or she learns and organizes information. The process of study is largely about organizing information so that it can be accessed and used efficiently.

The third finding deals with metacognition, or thinking about one's own thinking.

Finding 3

A metacognitive approach to instruction can help students learn to take control of their own learning by defining learning goals and monitoring their progress in achieving them.

Helping educators to develop a metacognitive approach to teaching and learning is the focus of this book. In future chapters we explore the definition of metacognition, provide examples of metacognitive thinking in a variety of contexts both within and outside of educational institutions, and provide educators with both food for thought and practical strategies for ensuring that their students not only pass mandated assessments during their education, but also become flexible, self-regulating learners who understand as well as remember and who can apply the taught curriculum flexibly and creatively in contexts beyond the classroom setting. The following definition of metacognition is developed in the next chapter and it is used throughout the book:

> Metacognition is the conscious application of an individual's thinking to their own thought processes with the specific intention of *understanding, monitoring, evaluating,* and *regulating* those processes.

By making ourselves aware of the processes of our thinking, we can monitor, evaluate, and regulate it as we move closer to our objectives.

We end this chapter with a discussion of what the brain does when it is concentrating on its own thought processes. As we have emphasized, it is important to pay attention to our thinking, especially when learning. Many of the things we think we have forgotten we actually never remembered because we were not paying attention to the learning process.

An important part of the brain's architecture is its division into two hemispheres—right and left. The left hemisphere is generally responsible for rational thought; it controls language, mathematics, abstraction, and reasoning. Memory in the left hemisphere is stored as language. The right hemisphere is generally responsible for emotion; it controls the visual and spatial senses, social skills, holistic thought, intuition, art, and music. Memory in the right hemisphere is stored nonlinguistically. The fact that memory is stored differently in each hemisphere underlies the need for using both linguistic and nonlinguistic thoughts in skillful learning. Why would we want to learn anything with only half a brain?

Information comes into your brain both from your observations, as sensory data, and from its internal monitoring of your body. This information comes into *sensory memory,* where it remains for 1 or 2 seconds before being discarded. About 90% of the information coming into the sensory memory is abandoned as irrelevant. For example, your big toe is constantly sending you information "I'm OK," and this information is promptly disregarded; but when you stub your big toe, the message changes, and you retain that information until you are finished dealing with the stub. Sense data is treated similarly; when you first notice the speaker at the dais you see he is wearing a carnation in his lapel and you may think about that for a few

| **Figure 2.2** | Schematic diagram of the initial inflow of information into the sensory memory. |

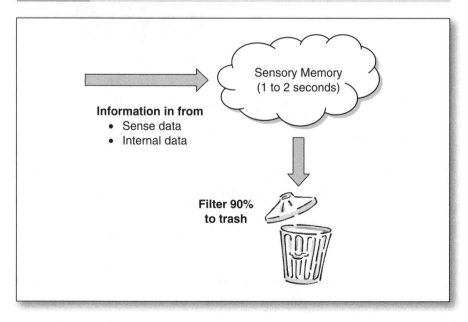

moments. Later, when you are listening to his speech, you still see the carnation but disregard it in favor of focusing on his message.

Your attention is required to keep information you wish to focus on in your mind. Your attention transfers information to *working memory,* where it may remain for about 18 seconds, unless you concentrate on keeping it there. Without an effort on your part, the information that is in the working memory will be replaced. By concentrating on thoughts in your working memory, you can focus on learning and transfer those thoughts to *short-term memory,* where it remains until transferred to your *long-term memory* as you sleep.

Figure 2.3 Schematic diagram of the internal flow of information in the brain.

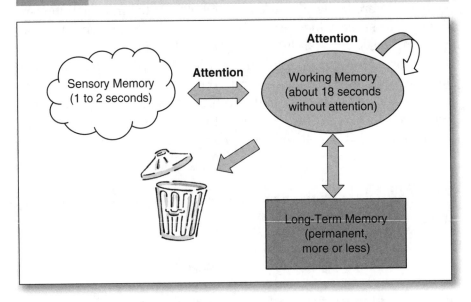

So we see that attention is required to retain thoughts in focus. But in addition to paying attention, there are three other important attributes of learning and remembering:

Observing. Observing is a basic skill involved in remembering. Often an observation (seeing, hearing, or feeling) is the first encounter with something we want to remember. It is often the case that what we think we have forgotten is simply what we didn't ever adequately observe in the first place.

Imagining. Imagining helps us remember by using nonlinguistic (right brain) as opposed to linguistic (left brain) representations.

Connecting. Linking images can help us to remember them, especially if one set of images is connected sequentially—for example, to a story—or if the images evoke some kind of emotional response.

You know the old joke: "'How do you get to Carnegie Hall?' 'Practice, practice, practice.'" The same applies to "How do I improve my memory?"—practice, practice, practice. Here are some exercises that can improve your memory. Do them every day; remember, "Practice, practice, practice." Set some time aside each day for mental exercise, and use it to plan your activities.

1. *Practice Observation.* Try to remember something you have seen during the day: for example, what someone you met earlier was wearing, what you heard on radio or TV, or the steps someone took to accomplish a task. When you encounter an interesting scene like a scenic view, a marketplace panorama, or part of a movie, make a conscious effort to remember the scene, and then, when you get home, write down all the detail you can remember.

2. *Create Images.* Pick a noun at random, such as *flower, table,* or *ship.* Now try to imagine that object. Embellish your image with details: a drop of dew on a rose, shadows of a bowl on a table, or background clouds illuminated by sunlight. Push yourself to imagine abstract nouns that do not represent objects—words like *stress, freedom,* or *love.*

3. *Connect Images.* Practice imagining images together. The connections can be logical or illogical, serious or whimsical, or they may be based on a specific sequence or acronym. Pick two objects at random (a chair and a towel, a tree and an elephant, or a needle and an automobile) and create an image involving them both. Try to create a logical connection between them, and then create an illogical or whimsical image.

We end this chapter with some general advice on how to maintain a healthy brain. There are many sources for information on this topic. One good general reference is John Ratey's *A User's Guide to the Brain* (2001). Practical information on brain health can be obtained in many places: for example, in works by Andrew Weil and Gary Small (2007).

Pay attention to your general health. The most important factor in keeping your brain healthy is to pay attention to your general health. Keep your body healthy. Eat well and exercise regularly. Avoid toxic substances that can affect your brain such as air pollution, smoking, excessive alcohol, and street drugs. Avoid injury by wearing protective gear such as seat belts and helmets when appropriate. Learn to manage stress. Get enough sleep.

Challenge your brain. It is important to challenge your brain to learn new and novel tasks, especially processes that you've never done before like learning a new language. Other activities that require new learning might include square dancing, chess, tai chi, yoga, or sculpture. Here are some suggestions for activities that will exercise your brain: crosswords, Sudoku, meeting new people and engaging in conversations, attending events different from your usual routine, trying new foods, cooking new recipes, reading a different genre of book, or watching a challenging movie and thinking about what it is that disconcerts you.

1. *Break routines.* Use the opposite hand when performing routine tasks like brushing your teeth or operating the TV remote. This exercise can strengthen neural connections and even create new ones. For example, switch the hand you are using to control the computer mouse. Use the hand you normally do *not* use. What do you notice? Is it harder to be precise and accurate with your motions? Don't worry if you are feeling uncomfortable and awkward; your brain is learning a new skill. Other ideas include going to work or to the store by a new route, eating with your nondominant hand, shopping at a new grocery, store or going through a certain (safe) portion of your daily routine with your eyes closed.

2. *Try to include one or more of your senses in an everyday task.* Get dressed with your eyes closed; wash your hair with your eyes closed; share a meal and use only visual cues to communicate (no talking).

3. *Combine two senses.* Listen to music and smell flowers; listen to the rain and tap your fingers; watch clouds and play with modeling clay at the same time.

4. *Travel.* Travel is another good way to stimulate your brain. It worked for our ancestors, the early *Homo sapiens.* Their nomadic lifestyle provided a tremendous stimulation for their brains that led to the development of superior tools and survival skills. Early humans gained a crucial evolutionary edge from the flexibility and innovation required by their strategic lifestyle, which also led to a more diverse diet that allowed their brains to rapidly evolve.

5. *Socialize.* Interacting with people in new or complex social settings is stimulating. Membership in clubs with an objective
   gives you an opportunity to exchange ideas and reflect on your
   thoughts and the thoughts of others.

With proper care and feeding of your brain, it should continue to
serve you well throughout your life.

Summary

- The extensive research on thinking and learning reported in
  How People Learn describes how an individual can come to a
  greater understanding of his or her own brain and its functions.
  Understanding how we learn should underpin everything we
  do in our educational institutions; it involves three important
  skills:
  - First is the need to recognize and respond to the individual's
    prior knowledge, both their preconceptions and their mis-
    conceptions.
  - Second, is the need to consider how that knowledge is orga-
    nized in the learner's brain and find ways to help students
    with this organization, so that they are able to link new
    learning with previous learning and transfer what is learned
    from one context to another.
  - Finally, and this is the focus of our book, is the need to
    understand the importance of metacognition to the develop-
    ment of creative, independent, lifelong learners.

THINKING DEEPER: DISCUSSION QUESTIONS

1. Think about one of the topics you are currently teaching to your students. What do you know about their preconceptions? Describe any
   misconceptions you have uncovered.

2. What do your students need to know and be able to do in order to successfully pass tests? Working with two or three others, create a networked structure that organizes these elements. You might begin by
   determining the most important elements and then looking for ways in
   which others are linked with those and then with each other.

3. When you cannot understand something at first, what do you do to
   develop your understanding?

3

Deconstructing Metacognition

Know thyself.

—inscription on the Temple of Apollo
at Delphi, ca. 500 BCE

Why Metacognition Is Important

The more our educational community learns about the human brain
and how it operates, the more important looms the idea that students
need to think about how they are thinking, especially as they are
learning. Metacognition, or thinking about one's own thinking,
emerges as a vital element of effective thought. In their recent book,
Learning and Leading with Habits of Mind, Art Costa and Bena Kallick
describe students lacking metacognitive skills as follows:

> Students often follow instructions or perform tasks without
> wondering why they are doing what they are doing. They
> seldom question themselves about their own learning strate-
> gies or evaluate the efficiency of their own performances.
> They have little or no motivation to do so. Some children
> virtually have no idea of what they should do when they

confront a problem and are often unable to explain their strategies of decision-making. For these children learning is reduced to episodic rote learning and memorization, primarily directed at passing tests and getting through school. And many of them do, but just barely. They can do better. (Costa & Kallick, 2008)

When a student's behavior is not heading in the right direction, we often say "Stop and think about what you are doing," and then help that student find an appropriate way of behaving. When a student's intellectual activity is not on track, we need to invoke a different exhortation, "Stop and think about what you are thinking," and then help the student find an appropriate way of thinking.

Recent research from several different fields has led to a new view of the human brain and points to the importance of students being actively involved in their learning. This active involvement includes the engagement of students' minds in the learning process. As we described in the previous chapter, pedagogical findings of brain research, summarized in a report by the United States National Academy of Science titled *How People Learn* (National Research Council, 2000), provides recommendations for teachers striving to have their students learn thoughtfully and skillfully. It describes the emerging understanding that effective learning requires personal introspection— a metacognition: *A metacognitive approach to instruction can help students learn to take control of their own learning by defining learning goals and monitoring their progress in achieving them.*

Helping students understand and control how they think is difficult. How does one guide students to an awareness of their own mental processes? How does one talk to students about what is going on in their minds? The content of a person's mind is, after all, known only to that person. We propose a language and a structure to formalize and facilitate understanding and speaking about metacognition. We intend here to analyze and clarify the constituents of metacognition so that teachers may find ways of including it among their own pedagogic strategies.

The ability to think skillfully and to reflect on our thinking is not an innate human characteristic. Some individuals develop metacognitive skills on their own, but usually in a haphazard manner. Furthermore, earlier research has shown that around 30% of the adult population never engages in metacognition (Chiabetta, 1976; Whimbey, 1980). Since understanding how to perform this kind of mental activity can significantly improve one's learning skills, teachers who can help students with this metacognition will increase the efficiency of their learning and thinking.

When we help students understand *how* their brains work and give them the strategies to make them work better, they are more likely to think effectively and skillfully and take control of their own learning. Carol Dweck of Stanford University divided struggling college students into two groups; both groups were taught basic study skills, but one group was given a series of classes explaining that intelligence is not a fixed entity but can, in fact, grow. When students adopted this "growth mindset," their learning improved.

At the end of the semester, the students with study skills alone had not applied what they had learned, and their grades had continued to decline. The other group showed significant improvement in their grades, and other teachers were able to identify the students who had had the growth model lessons from those who had not (Dweck, 2008).

It is important for teachers and students to become aware of these emerging views about intelligence, because when individuals realize they can improve their processes of learning and thinking, they most often choose to do so. Skillful thinking and learning make knowledge more useful and transportable and can initiate a lifelong process of continual development of the brain.

What Is Cognition?

In order to understand metacognition (thinking about one's own thinking) we must first have a clear notion of cognition—thinking. Edward de Bono has defined thinking as *the deliberate exploration of experience for a purpose* (de Bono, 1976).

It is useful to elaborate on this definition by scrutinizing each of the important words in it. The action of thinking is an *exploration*, so when one thinks, one investigates, studies, examines, or analyzes. The object explored when thinking is one's *experience*, that is, the collection of events that make up one's conscious life. The domain of an individual's thought is the entire content of that person's conscious mind. Furthermore, this exploration of experience is *deliberate*, which implies that the action is performed carefully and thoroughly. Finally, the action is carried out for a *purpose*, so there is some goal or aspiration to attain. Thus thinking is a careful and thorough investigation of one's conscious mind in order to achieve a specific objective.

Thinking may be as simple as trying to recollect who was present at your 16th birthday party, or as complex as your reflections on finding meaning in your life. In thinking (cognition), we function in two different but interrelated modes. One mode deals with a cognitive skill—the type of thinking being used. How we think depends on the purpose of our thinking. We think differently when trying to remember a friend's birth date (*When is Sally's birthday?*) than when we speculate on the outcome of our action (*What will happen if I forget Sally's birthday?*). We may be thinking by sorting through a list and trying to classify the items in it, or we may be working through a deductive reasoning process (if . . . then . . .) to decide on a course of action.

There are many descriptions of cognitive skills and lists of the different types of thinking. Perhaps the most familiar to educators is Bloom's taxonomy and its more recent derivatives (Bloom, 1956). Table 3.1

Table 3.1 A Revision of Bloom's Taxonomy

Cognitive Skill	Description	Cognitive Subskills
Remember	retrieve relevant knowledge from long-term memory	Recognizing Recalling
Understand	construct meaning, build connections between prior knowledge and new knowledge, integrate new knowledge with existing schemas and cognitive frameworks	Interpreting Exemplifying Classifying Summarizing Inferring Comparing Explaining
Apply	use procedures to perform exercises or solve problems (use procedural knowledge)	Executing Implementing
Analyze	break information into its constituent parts, determine how the parts are related to each other and to an overall structure	Differentiating Organizing Attributing
Evaluate	make judgments based on criteria and standards	Checking Critiquing
Create	reorganize elements into a new pattern or structure	Generating Planning Producing

Source: Adapted from Mayer (2001).

describes a revision of Bloom's taxonomy by Richard Mayer. This revision modifies the 6 primary cognitive skills originally introduced by Bloom and adds 19 subskills or cognitive processes.

For example, when using the cognitive skill of *evaluation*, one makes judgments based on criteria and standards; the subskill of *checking* (or *coordinating, detecting, monitoring,* or *testing*) involves judgments about internal consistency, and the subskill of *critiquing* (or *judging*) involves judgments based on external criteria. The table of this revised taxonomy provides a simple list of the ways in which we think. It is useful because it provides a structure for thinking about the cognitive process as well as providing a language to discuss it with others. We include a more comprehensive list of cognitive skills in Table 3.5 (at the end of this chapter) based on the work of Robert Swartz, Director of the National Center for Teaching Thinking (Swartz, 2001).

The other mode of thinking involves how we conduct ourselves in support of our thought, or our personal behavior while thinking. It encompasses such dispositions as persistence, striving for accuracy, gathering data effectively, or thinking flexibly. How we behave while thinking is an important attribute of our thought process. Our behavior when working alone is different from our behavior when working as part of a team; it is different when we are gathering data from when we are thinking creatively. A good list of these behaviors is the Habits of Mind compiled by Arthur Costa and Bena Kallick. Costa and Kallick have studied the behavior patterns of successful people and distilled them into a set of 16 dispositions or habits (Costa & Kallick, 2000).

As educators, Costa and Kallick were motivated to offer guidance to teachers striving to provide their students with the best practices to achieve skillful thinking. Table 3.2 shows the Habits of Mind; we discuss them individually in the following two chapters. Again, this list describes the structure of conduct supporting thinking and provides a language to discuss it.

Thus, thinking is a careful examination of our mind to achieve a specific purpose. When thinking skillfully, we employ one or more of the cognitive tasks listed in Table 3.1 (or Table 3.5 at the end of the chapter) and we conduct ourselves according to one or more of the Habits of Mind. Clearly, a skillful thinker is able to discriminate and make appropriate choices among these cognitive skills and behaviors.

Table 3.2   Habits of Mind

Personal Traits	Acquiring Information
Persisting	Gathering data through all senses
Managing impulsivity	Listening with understanding and empathy
Striving for accuracy	Questioning and posing problems
Finding humor	Remaining open to continuous learning
Thinking Tools	Response to Thought
Thinking flexibly	Creating, imagining, innovating
Thinking and communicating with clarity and precision	Responding with wonderment and awe
Thinking interdependently	Thinking about thinking (metacognition)
Applying past knowledge to new situations	Taking responsible risks

Source: Adapted from Costa and Kallick (2000).

What is Metacognition?

What then is metacognition—the thinking about one's thinking? We introduce the following definition:

> Metacognition is the conscious application of an individual's thinking to their own thought processes with the specific intention of *understanding, monitoring, evaluating,* and *regulating* those processes.

Metacognition is a conscious examination of one's thinking; an individual must be aware that the focus of their thinking is on their own thought processes in order for metacognition to take place. The purpose of metacognition is one or more of the four intentions listed in the definition.

These intentions represent increasingly more sophisticated stages of metacognition (Swartz, 2001).The first intention of metacognition is *understanding,* which implies an awareness that one's thinking is directed toward one's own thought processes. The second intention, *monitoring,* is checking to see that the thinking is on the right track. This includes an awareness of the two modalities of thought: the type of thinking being used and the disposition of the thinker toward those thoughts and their consequences. Are the results of the thinking reasonable? Is the right type of thinking being used? Are appropriate habits of mind exercised? The third intention, *evaluation*, involves an assessment of how well the thinking is proceeding toward its objective. The final intention, *regulation*, involves adjusting the thought process to make sure the objective is attained and then reviewing the thinking and modifying the thought process so that it will be even more effective the next time it is used.

Edward de Bono developed a metaphor for intelligence in order to dispel the myth that your intelligence limits how well you can think. As we know there are various kinds of cars; some are powerful, like a Ferrari, and others not so powerful, like a Volkswagen. The way a particular car is driven depends equally on the characteristics of the car and the skill of the driver. An experienced driver can maneuver a Volkswagen more skillfully than an inexperienced driver at the wheel of a Ferrari. Similarly, there are various powers of the human brain. Your intelligence, de Bono says, is analogous to the power in a car; it may be a Ferrari or it may be a Volkswagen. However, its utility to you depends on how well you learn to "drive" it. According to de Bono, "Thinking is the driving skill with which each individual drives his or her intelligence." If we extend the metaphor, the more skillfully we drive the Volkswagen, the more closely it comes to approximating a Ferrari! Like all metaphors, this one has flaws; human intelligence is not as static as a car's power but, in fact, can be improved with conscious effort (de Bono, 1994a, 1994b).

We can expand this metaphor by noting that you can be a driver of any car without knowing how that car works. However, your knowledge of how the car works can help you be a better driver. Developing your skill at thinking is like learning to be a driver who understands the car being driven. Thinking about how you are thinking and controlling your brain is like incorporating your knowledge of how a car operates into your driving techniques. For example, a driver may be skilled at shifting gears manually under ordinary circumstances; however, understanding what happens physically when the gears are shifted can help decide how to shift in difficult terrain. The ability to drive safely on a wet and twisting road is enhanced by an understanding of tires and traction. Metacognition is like knowing how your brain works and incorporating that knowledge into how you think. It is particularly valuable when the "thinking terrain" gets rough or slippery—when one is faced with problems whose solutions are not immediately or easily discovered.

What Are the Objects of Metacognition?

So if metacognition is thinking about our own thinking, how do we go about it? First let us consider what we might be thinking about when we think about our own thinking. What does one think about when one ponders one's thoughts?

We have seen that thinking—ordinary cognition—involves two modes, one relating to the cognitive skill being used and the other relating to our conduct in support of thinking. When we think about our thinking we can think about these two modes, but in addition our thoughts can also turn to the content of our thoughts. For example, if a student is thinking about a concept in physics, then she can think about how her brain is dealing with that concept using the language of physics. In metacognition involving the content from an academic discipline one can think about one's thoughts using the language of that discipline; metacognition about a sport uses the language of that sport. Thus, there are three general objects of metacognition: (1) the *content* of our thoughts, (2) the *cognitive skills* being used, and (3) our *conduct* in support of thinking. These are depicted in Table 3.3; we will examine them individually.

Table 3.3   Objects of Metacognition

Objects of Metacognition	Objectives (reasons to metacogitate)	Language
Content—what one is thinking about	to monitor understanding of concepts or track progress in problem solving or formulating plans	Discipline
Cognition—type of thinking being used	to achieve the objective of one's thinking and to sharpen thinking skills	Types of thinking
Conduct—personal behavior supporting thinking	to develop the habits of a successful thinker	Habits of Mind

The Content of Thought (What am I thinking about?)

When we think about our thinking, we sometimes need to focus on the content of our thought—that is, just what we are thinking about right now. It might be knowledge we already possess as we try to recall some specific information, a concept we are trying to understand, a problem we are trying to solve, or a plan we are trying to formulate. We can think about our thoughts as we are thinking of them. The reason for metacognition about the content of our thought is to monitor our own understanding of concepts involved, to track our progress toward the objective of thought, or to check for consistency with other knowledge.

The Cognitive Skill Being Used (How should I think about it?)

Sometimes we may need to think about the cognitive skill being used; that is, the type of thinking we are engaged in to achieve our goal. Should I be listing, describing, comparing, or evaluating? The objective of metacognition about the cognitive skill being used is to ensure that the right thinking skills are brought to bear on the problem at hand and to sharpen these skills for future use. We may also need to seek alternative means of reaching or justifying our conclusions.

Personal Behavior Supporting Thinking (What dispositions should I adopt while thinking?)

In addition to the thoughts running through one's mind, one may also reflect on specific behaviors supporting the thinking. How diligent is the thinker? Is the thinker using all available resources? The objective of metacognition about one's behavior is to develop these behaviors into the habits of a successful thinker. Am I activating Habits of Mind that best support the purpose of my thinking? Table 3.4 summarizes the objectives and intentions of metacognition.

Strategies for Incorporating Metacognition Into Practice

Understanding Metacognition

In order to develop the ability to use metacognition effectively, students need to understand it and be able to speak about it. Young children, even preschoolers, have demonstrated the ability to perform simple metacognitive tasks (Butterfield & Ferretti, 1987; Flavell, Friedrichs, & Hoyt, 1970). Furthermore, as they grow, children's

Table 3.4 The Metacognitive Process

Objects of Metacognition	Intentions of Metacognition			
	Understand	*Monitor*	*Evaluate*	*Regulate*
Content of the Thought	Do I recognize that I am thinking about my thinking?	Am I able to check the reasonableness of my ideas and the progress of my thinking?	Do I understand well enough? Is the result correct and consistent with my other knowledge?	Can I now use this knowledge flexibly? Can I now act on this knowledge? If not, what need I do?
Types of Thinking Being Used	Do I recognize the type of thinking I am using?	Am I using the right mix of my thinking skills?	Am I using these skills effectively enough?	Did I use this skill well? Can I improve on my thinking the next time I use these skills?
Personal Behavior Supporting Thinking	Do I recognize the behaviors that contribute to the success or failure of my thought and its consequences?	Am I using the right habits of mind? What other behavior should I bring to bear?	Am I using these habits well enough to achieve my objectives?	How might I behave when facing similar problems in the future?

knowledge base increases, and so does their ability to monitor that knowledge (Schneider, 1985). There is growing evidence that young children can learn metacognition and that this ability facilitates subsequent learning (National Research Council, 2000).

For effective, lasting learning to take place, students must also understand the levels of metacognitive thought. These levels were first introduced by David Perkins and Robert Swartz (Swartz, 2001). They correspond closely to the intentions of metacognition (as one grows in the ability to think about thinking, one's metacognition grows in sophistication). These require that metacognitive thinkers

1. be aware of the kinds of thinking they are doing (*understand*),

2. know the strategies they are using to do the thinking (*monitor*),

3. reflectively evaluate the effectiveness of their thinking (*evaluate*), and

4. plan how they would do some similar kind thinking in the future (*regulate*).

Looking for Opportunities

Opportunities for metacognition can be interwoven into every lesson. One effective technique for this is Think Aloud Problem Solving (Costa & Kallick, 2000), in which students are invited to

1. describe their plans and strategies for solving the problem,

2. share their thinking as they are implementing their plan,

3. reflect on/evaluate the effectiveness of their strategy, and

4. plan the best strategy for the next similar thinking task.

Costa points out that metacognition is engaged and sustained in teaching when the teacher

- encourages students to check for accuracy by asking students questions such as
  o "How do you know you are right?"
  o "What other ways can you prove that you are correct?"
- creates opportunities for students to clarify
  o "Explain what you mean when you said 'you just figured it out.'"
  o "When you said you started at the beginning, how did you know where to begin?"
- provides data, not answers, when students are on the wrong track or confused
  o "I think you heard it wrong; let me repeat the question."
  o "You need to check your observations or data."
- resists making judgments
  o "So, your hypothesis is . . . ?"
  o "Who has a different thought?"
- makes sure students stay focused on thinking
  o "Tell us what strategies you used to solve that problem."
- encourages persistence
  o "I know you can do this. Let's try another approach."

If we want our students to think metacognitively, it is important that we spend time exploring answers to the question "How did you find that out?" or "How did you work that out?" Students can learn from understanding how others found different paths to the same solution. If the class has a particularly productive discussion on the various solutions to a problem, ask them to work out a simple statement of the solution as a final step.

Students from kindergarten to college will come across words in their reading with which they are unfamiliar. A metacognitive reader always begins untangling this problem by asking the question "What makes sense here?" Younger students can then use their graphophonic knowledge to discriminate between possibilities, and older students can look for further references to confirm their hunches or provide additional information.

Fifteen minutes at the end of the school day writing in a learning journal can provide insight into both what has been learned and how it was learned. Initially, you will need to give guidance about the sorts of things to write, but in time students become self-sufficient and grow in their insight. This can be done with students from Grade 1 to Grade 12. At the end of each day, ask your students "What do you know now that you didn't know when you arrived this morning?" and "When did you behave intelligently today?" These questions can start rich discussions with students of all ages.

Self-evaluation is another powerful metacognitive tool.

We have provided a Metacognitive Monitor in the Resources section of the book to help students to focus on the *how* of learning rather than on the *what*, as we have traditionally done.

Very young students can simply draw a face with a smile, a frown, or a neutral look at the conclusion of a piece of work to indicate their progress. Allow students to read three other students' work without comment and then reevaluate their own work. This provides them with a yardstick, in addition to the rubrics and standards provided by the teacher, with which to measure their own performance. On the other hand, they may want to keep their self-evaluation private; but even this should result in a clearly articulated single strategy to be employed next time that will improve their own work. Give the students opportunities to share these strategies.

Extended peer evaluation is a metacognitive tool that enables the older student to assess and adapt learning strategies that may not be working well. When students have nearly finished a final draft of an essay, have them exchange essays, either randomly or with teacher direction. Each student reads another student's draft essay and makes constructive criticisms on a separate piece of paper. The essays are then passed on to a second person, who repeats the process. Finally the essay is returned to the writer with both sets of constructive criticism. By thinking interdependently, each student now has the benefit of two other points of view. By assessing the value of these additional sources, the student can assess his own thinking and adjust the first draft as needed. By reading the drafts of two other students, opportunities have been created for new learning that might cause a student to rethink his initial work.

Using the Language

The language of metacognition should be used to make the thinking involved in learning experiences more explicit. If you want students to make comparisons, instead of saying "Let's look at these pictures," make the cognitive task involved explicit by saying "Let's compare these pictures." Instead of asking what will happen if a certain action is performed, ask the students to predict what will happen if that act is performed. Similarly, make the behavioral aspects of Habits of Mind clear—for example, by saying "As we begin to discuss our work so far, let's remember to listen to each other with empathy and understanding."

Teaching the Skills

It is not enough to tell students that "today we will be comparing and contrasting." We cannot assume that students know how to carry out the cognitive tasks if we have not taught them how. Time must be set aside to explicitly teach the skill using the content of the curriculum. Students need to understand and be able to use the subskills that make up each of these cognitive tasks at a level appropriate to their stage of development.

Similarly, it is not enough to tell students they should be persistent without also telling them how. Persistence is not about repeatedly banging one's head against the wall. It requires having a range of different strategies to fall back on when the first one doesn't work. It involves being able to change one's point of view and look at a problem from a different angle. Persistent people are aware of the range of resources available to them and they know how to make use of them. Students need to learn the subskills that make persistence and the other Habits of Mind possible.

Integrating Metacognition in the Planning

Use metacognition in planning lessons. A simple way to integrate metacognitive exercises into existing curricula is to make sure that the start of every lesson includes a description of what *content, cognition,* and *conduct* will be emphasized in the lesson. It is a common practice to spell out the content of the lesson: "Today we will review two physical characteristics of an object, its mass and volume, and then introduce the concept of density." It is probably less common practice to describe the cognitive skills involved in the lesson. "When we do our work today, we will classify various objects by comparing and contrasting their properties and then predict their density." This can be followed by a description of the conduct that will be useful to use during the work. "We will be working in teams, so working interdependently and thinking and communicating with accuracy and precision will be important."

Kindergarten to University

At our professional development workshops on the Habits of Mind, we are often asked if very young children, especially kindergarten and first grade students, can really understand and use the Habits. This is an important question because teachers want to make sure their effort is effective and that their instructional strategies really work. Metacognition is perhaps the most complex Habit, so let's look at it. We need not necessarily employ this particular term with our youngest students but instead could refer to it as "thinking about their thinking." The exhortation "Put on your thinking caps" is a familiar attempt to get students aware of their thinking. So we pose the question, "Can very young children understand and control their thinking processes?"

First, the research shows that, in fact, even infants demonstrate metacognition at their level of thinking. This question has been studied ever since the term *metacognition* was introduced by Flavell. Preschoolers have demonstrated the ability to perform simple metacognitive tasks (Butterfield & Ferretti, 1987; Flavell et al., 1970). Furthermore, as they grow, children's knowledge base increases and so does their ability to monitor that knowledge (Schneider, 1985). There continues to be evidence that young children can learn metacognition and that this ability facilitates subsequent learning (National Research Council, 2000).

It is important to remember that the ability to reflect on our thinking is not an innately well-developed human characteristic, so if children can be introduced to metacognitive skills at an early age, their learning throughout life will be enhanced.

Research aside, perhaps the best way to demonstrate children's understanding of metacognition is by an example. We offer one which came to us as a surprise and still remains a delight to remember. We were working recently with a cluster of schools in New South Wales, Australia, and visited a small rural school classroom of preparatory, first grade, and second grade students. Pat eagerly accepted the teacher's offer to teach a lesson in mathematics. She introduced a game that she had used often in her own classrooms. It is a mathematics game where counters are placed into and taken out of a closed container (in this instance, Pat's pocket). She told the children, "I'm putting in six, now I'm taking out two, now I'm putting in two groups of two" and so on. The children are expected to keep the calculation going in their heads until the teacher asks "How many counters are in my pocket?" After playing this game a few times, we then asked the children a metacognitive question: "What was happening in your brains as you got to your answer?" A five-year-old said, "I could see the counters in my brain going in and coming out. When you finished, I counted how many were left." A first grade student told us, "I saw a number line in my head and kept moving on the number line." A second grader explained that he remembered learning number facts and used those.

Because their teacher regularly focuses questions on thinking rather than solely on the correct answer, these children have come to understand that there are a number of different ways to solve a variety of learning tasks. Their teacher understood the importance of metacognition to learning, and so these very young students were used to talking about *how* they learned as well as describing *what* they had learned.

There are two observations we can draw from this story. First, if children are guided to think about their own thoughts, they can then evaluate their own thinking, which is the first step toward improving it. Second, an open classroom discussion about how a particular question was resolved allows students to see how other students approach the same problem and gives children the opportunity to increase their own range of thinking strategies. This argues for introducing the process of metacognition early, so that children's thinking skills can develop with their learning from their earliest school days.

The ability to think metacognitively is what enables us to monitor and improve the skill with which we think. Metacognition can be learned, and so it is important that educators understand how to teach it explicitly as an integrated part of any curriculum.

Summary

The ability to think metacognitively is a foundation of successful learning. Thinking about our own thinking needs to be explicitly taught. When we engage in metacognition, we are consciously examining our own thought processes in order to understand the kinds of thinking we are using in a particular context. As we recognize the modes of thinking we are using, we can begin to assess their effectiveness and regulate or adjust them as necessary. There are three objects of metacognition. First, we need to be aware of *what* we are thinking about (the content): I am thinking about a quadratic equation, the motivations of Macbeth, or what I am going to do for dinner tonight. Second, we need to be aware of *how* we are thinking (the particular thinking skill we are using): are we surveying, evaluating, describing, and so on? Third, we need to consider the behaviors that will support our thinking: do I need to consult, persevere a little longer, obtain more data, and the like? The intentional teaching of metacognition needs to be embedded in both the language and the practices of the classroom.

THINKING DEEPER: DISCUSSION QUESTIONS

1. When you participate in a professional discussion group, what is the content of your thinking? How many different kinds of thinking might you be most likely to engage in?

2. What kinds of behaviors best support a fruitful and interesting discussion group?

3. After administering a test, consider the ways in which you could make it possible for your students to be able to identify and modify their thinking in order to perform better next time.

Table 3.5 Levels of Cognitive Abstraction

First Order Abstraction Processing Ideas	Second Order Abstraction Evaluating Ideas	Third Order Abstraction Metacognition

1. Treating facts or ideas as independent entities
   remembering
   accumulating facts
   generating new ideas
 	
2. Simple analysis of collections of facts or ideas
   classify
   sequence
   compare/contrast
   analogy/metaphor
   parts/whole reasoning
   reacting to intellectual input
 	
3. More complex analysis
   inference
      causal reasoning
      generalization
      prediction
      analogical reasoning
   summarizing
   deduction
      conditional (if . . . then)
      categorical (some . . . all)
   induction
 	
4. Complex cognitive tasks (systematic thinking)
   decision making
   planning
   calculating
   problem solving
      making assumptions or
      order of magnitude estimates
   speculating (What happens if . . . ?)
   modeling and simulation
	1. Assessing the reasonableness of ideas
	   assessing the reliability of information
	      the accuracy of observation
	      the reliability of sources
	
	2. Evaluating the utility of ideas
	
	3. Testing conclusions with reality
	   uncovering and evaluating assumptions
	   hypothesis and testing
	   identifying reasons and conclusions
	
	4. Reformulating ideas based upon assessment
	   (thesis, antithesis, synthesis)
	
	5. Evaluation of the human element in thinking
	   with others
	      consensus
	      argumentation
	   with self
	      intuition
	      personal feelings
	      affective domain (emotions)
	
	6. Self-directed inquiry
	   curiosity-based learning
		1. *Understand*—Being aware of the kind of thinking you are doing.
		
		2. *Monitor*—Knowing the thinking strategy you are using.
		
		3. *Evaluate*—Evaluating the effectiveness of your thinking.
		
		4. *Regulate*—Planning how you will do the same kind of thinking the next time it is needed.

Source: Adapted from the work of Arthur Costa and Bena Kallick, developers of Habits of Mind, and Robert Swartz, Director of the National Center for Teaching

4

Behaving Metacognitively

Habits of Mind

Habits are at first cobwebs, then cables.

—Spanish proverb

One of the objects of metacognition is the behavior we engage in as learners to support our thinking. When we examine these behaviors, when we understand them and are able to assess their effectiveness, and when we can then modify less productive behaviors, we are behaving metacognitively.

When striving to achieve any complex goal, we need to think about what we are doing and how we are progressing toward that goal. We constantly encounter situations that require thought before action, and if we have developed a set of strategies to use in these situations, we are able to act more effectively. People who are consistently successful in their endeavors develop habits or dispositions to support their objectives. Art Costa and Bena Kallick examined the habits of successful people in a wide range of walks of life and synthesized a list of 16 dispositions that support successful thinking and acting. These Habits of Mind help us work through our problems.

There are many resources describing the Habits of Mind and how they can be introduced in the classroom. These resources include the original books by Costa and Kallick (2000), and an updated book by these authors (2008). A recent publication by James Anderson (2010) describes the implementation of the Habits in Australia. There are also several online resources that include lesson plans submitted by teachers, posters, and exercises.[1] In this chapter we describe the Habits individually, and in the following chapter we offer an example of how they can be used to solve important problems. There are many ways in which we might want to organize these Habits, but for convenience, we have divided the 16 Habits of Mind into four groups of four as shown in Table 3.2.

When we encounter these Habits of Mind for the first time, they seem quite familiar but there is, in fact, an underlying complexity to each of them that requires an effort to understand. As we think more deeply about the behaviors that support successful thinking, we are thinking metacognitively. The reward for this effort is a significant increase in the sophistication of one's thinking. The ability to use the Habits evolves with the experience of using them thoughtfully. When the Habits are well understood, they are drawn on spontaneously in many different situations, and the sophistication of their application increases with use.

Individuals need to recognize the value inherent in developing the Habits of Mind as a positive contribution to their effective thinking and then commit themselves to a lifelong effort of continuous improvement in the way they think. Let us now examine the 16 Habits of Mind one by one.

Personal Traits

Persisting

Persisting means sticking to a task until it is completed. To be persistent, one must have a clearly articulated objective and remain focused on that objective until it is achieved. There must be a plan or strategy to reach that objective. The plan must be flexible enough to accommodate unexpected situations, and alternative strategies should be available in case some strategies prove to be ineffective. It may be necessary to break a complex objective into stages with clear objectives for each stage leading to the ultimate goal. There must be some means of measuring progress toward the objective and assessing the effectiveness of the strategy being used. When a learner gets stuck in attempting to solve a mathematical problem, persistence is only feasible if the learner has alternative strategies to draw upon. That's why it is so important for teachers to ensure that their students explore a variety of ways to solve learning problems. Skill-building exercises in which students repeat a process multiple times until they have achieved a high level of proficiency have their place, but not at the expense of discovering alternative strategies. The question "Could we have done this in another way?" is powerful.

Managing Impulsivity

Managing impulsivity means knowing when to pause and reflect before acting and when to respond quickly and decisively. In many situations, it is better to think before acting, to gather the information needed to decide on a course of action, to reflect on alternatives, and to be sure that the problem is clearly understood. Thinking before acting can help to avoid errors resulting from premature action. In other cases, it is necessary to react decisively and creatively. Much inappropriate behavior in the school and in the home is the result of poor impulse management, but creative thought can suffer when impulse control is too strict and the spontaneous qualities of thought are lost. Dealing with the situation when someone cuts in line ahead of you requires very different impulse management skills from contributing to a free-flowing, explorative brainstorming session.

Striving for Accuracy and Precision

Striving for accuracy and precision means working to achieve a quality outcome. It requires careful attention to detail, keeping the margins of error as small as possible, and fully understanding the implications of any inaccuracy. It involves checking and assessing the accuracy of information being used and not always accepting the conventional wisdom but testing all information for consistency. An important part of striving for accuracy is recognizing that knowledge is often not absolute and that uncertainty is the constant companion of those seeking new knowledge. Consequently, uncertainty needs to be regularly assessed. The question "How do you know you are right?" is another powerful question.

Finding Humor

Humor appears to be a unique attribute of human beings. It is capable of producing beneficial psychological and physiological effects.

To find humor in a situation requires the ability to understand that situation and to view it from differing perspectives. Humor provides a leveling to the rise and fall of fortunes in any enterprise. Much humor has its roots in our ability to recognize and delight in the unexpected.

Humor shares an important characteristic with lateral thinking. Lateral thinking involves moving away from a familiar pathway (dominant paradigm) to an alternative path. A good joke leads the listener down a path until the punch line shifts to another, surprising path. Humor helps us look at things differently.

Acquiring Information

Gathering Data Through All Senses

The brain gathers and coordinates sensory information from both inside and outside the body. People who are skilled at sensing and interpreting all of these varied data are able to understand and manage their surroundings better. Often, secondary senses provide important information—a person's facial expression can communicate as much as their spoken word, and holding an object in your hands can augment its visual examination. We learn better when all our senses are involved. We also know that different people have different preferred sensory pathways for their own learning. Some of us learn better if we hear a new concept explained, others need to read it to really understand it, and others need to write it down or draw a diagram before they assimilate the new learning.

Listening to Others With Understanding and Empathy

According to Stephen Covey, highly effective people take the time and effort to listen carefully to what others are telling them. This attention to the ideas and feelings of others improves the quality of communication and the information gathered. Understanding the viewpoints and feelings of others is important to understanding what they are trying to communicate. Often, paraphrasing the ideas of others enhances the conversation and keeps it on track. How many times have you been in a conversation where you sensed that the other person was simply waiting until you had finished speaking so they could continue with their train of thought? How easy it is to be distracted by things around us or the thoughts in our own minds instead of remaining focused on what the other person is saying. How much of what your conversational partner is saying do you miss because you are busy formulating your own next contribution? Listening is a tough business, and we need to keep our wits about us if we are to do it well.

Questioning and Posing Problems

The focus of this Habit is the development of an inquiring mind; that is, an awareness of when to ask questions and how to ask the kind of constructive questions that advance one's thinking. Posing questions is an important part of problem solving. It is critical to gathering necessary information and assessing the validity of that information.

In particular, when facing problems in which the initial steps required for solving them are not obvious, asking the right questions can lead to a clear starting point. Questioning along the way can keep you on a productive path toward a solution. The three Habits, *Listening with understanding and empathy, Thinking and communicating with clarity and precision,* and *Questioning and posing problems,* are companions; they are each acquired skills, and we will revisit them in more detail in Chapter 9.

Remaining Open to Continuous Learning

An individual's mind develops throughout his or her life; this Habit encourages a mindset always open to new knowledge. It requires a willingness to think about all of our experiences and mentally incorporate these experiences. This is the antithesis to "Don't confuse me with facts; I've made up my mind." Your brain is not an encyclopedia filled with a collection of facts, nor is it a set of instruction manuals. It is an organ in constant flux. Some pathways become deeply etched like ruts in a snow field and can be hard to escape. These habitual tracks can be both advantageous and disadvantageous, but with effort we can often escape from the ruts that lead us into trouble or dead ends and forge new tracks. The brain is a network of pathways, and as we learn we have the opportunity to form and reform them, creating new links and interconnections. Understanding that new learning can take place from the cradle to the grave is a powerful thing.

In Chapter 2, we have described the differences in thought processes of novices (unpracticed and episodic learners) and experts (those who have developed flexible and transferable expertise). We have stressed the significance of a personal awareness of how information is organized in our brains. This awareness is vital to insuring that new knowledge is organized so that it can be easily transferred to situations different from those in which it was learned. Acquisition of knowledge should not just be the episodic remembering of isolated facts but the continual development of a network of concepts.

Thinking Tools

Thinking Flexibly

Sometimes, when facing routine tasks, our thinking follows familiar patterns. Other situations dictate that we must adapt new and innovative methods of thinking. We can distinguish between *routine thinking,* in which a standard response follows the recognition of a familiar situation, and *adaptive thinking,* when new ways of thinking must be invoked. Edward de Bono coined the term *lateral thinking* for this latter mode of thinking away from the usual or routine pattern. The ability to think flexibly underlies a number of the other Habits of Mind. The ability to persist is dependent on the ability to find other ways around a difficulty when we seem to hit the wall. Humor grows out of the recognition of a path different from the expected. A good listener is able to stick with the ideas of another person even when they are in conflict with his own. It takes flexibility to see things from another person's perspective, and empathy is entirely dependent on the ability to do just that. The Habits of Mind are not isolated concepts. Like the brain itself, they form a network of intersecting and mutually supportive behaviors.

Chapter 7, on problem solving, analyzes lateral thinking and describes several techniques for thinking about problems in different ways. These techniques can be learned by anyone and do improve with practice.

Thinking and Communicating With Clarity and Precision

Imagine the pilot of the space shuttle guiding that huge machine from orbit to a safe landing. During that process, the pilot must assess the situation and communicate with her onboard crew and with the ground-based control center. The pilot's thinking must be clear and precise, as must her communication with others. When John Swigert on Apollo 13 said, "Houston, we have a problem," he didn't leave it there. What followed was a series of precise and clear exchanges that eventually led to the successful return of the space module and its crew to earth.

This Habit involves avoiding fuzzy thinking and vague speech, replacing vague statements like "It was big" with the more accurate "It was 4.2 meters in length." It's a Habit that seems to become particularly important during adolescence, when teenagers often appear to sink into a language of grunts, shrugs, and gestures. The use of stereotypes, overgeneralizations, and absolute statements are often examples of this fuzzy thinking. "But Mom, everyone has one of these" is heard from the mouths of our children very often, and a little adept parental questioning can reveal truth by focusing on clarity and precision: "Who else has one? Do you have any friends who don't have one?" Such questioning can also lead your child to communicate with greater clarity and precision and, with any luck, preserve a little of your bank balance.

This Habit involves striving to use appropriate language with attention to definitions, providing support for claims made, and specification of uncertainty. The process of writing forces thought into words and helps to expose faulty logic. It is a good way to practice clear and precise thinking and communicating. Asking a student to explain a newly learned concept to a partner not only helps the other student to learn, it also reveals to the first student the gaps and misunderstandings in his own mind. It is when we try to explain something that we best discover if we really understand it.

Thinking Interdependently

Thinking interdependently involves developing the inclination and ability to work with others. It requires us to recognize the social nature of humans and to acknowledge the fact that productivity often increases by working in groups. It ranges from willingness to seek advice to understanding the social dynamics of working in teams.

Working in teams requires several of the other Habits: *Listening with understanding and empathy, Questioning and posing problems*, and *Thinking and communicating with clarity and precision.* In addition, good teamwork requires understanding the elements of teamwork: The team acknowledges that it has a common goal, each member has specific tasks for which he or she is accountable, and each member has the ability to lead or to follow as required.

Technology provides new ways of working interdependently which, in turn, require new ways of thinking interdependently. The Internet has provided us with easy access to enormous quantities of information. Today we can even use our cell phones to "Google" something of which we are unsure. We can also bring the minds of total strangers across the entire globe to bear on our particular problems. We can share knowledge and information in a variety of online forums on an almost limitless range of subjects; for example, we can join a forum of photographers and learn from the experiences and expertise of the other members of that forum. We have unparalleled opportunities to think interdependently.

Applying Past Knowledge to New Situations

Clearly, when we face new, complex problems, we have no recourse but to draw on our past experience and transfer what we know into the new situation. The key to this Habit is to develop techniques for organizing knowledge so that it is transferable. We must anticipate that knowledge we acquire in one context may be used in various other contexts. Learning facts in isolation from one another or viewing our experience as separate episodes does not accomplish this. The key is to integrate what we learn.

It is a worrying trend that even in our earliest years of schooling we are dividing learning up into separate compartments so that our youngest children come to see history as separate from art, science as distinct from English, and social studies as separate from music. Instead, we should be striving for the integration of learning. Deep understanding of developments in art rely upon an awareness of the historical context, so it is important that we align curriculum across disciplines, enabling them to support each other. Teachers who work in cross-disciplinary teams have the opportunity to discuss ways in which the things students have already learned in mathematics can support the next unit in science, or the music teacher can explore the culture of the people in the parts of the world the students have focused on in geography.

One way in which this Habit manifests itself is in an individual's understanding of underlying concepts as opposed to just knowing a sequence of facts. Finding a context for new knowledge enhances one's ability to draw on it in various new situations. If, at the time of learning a series of facts, one seeks to find a principle that unifies them, these facts are more likely to be remembered in connection with that unifying principle.

Personal Responses to Thought

Creating, Imagining, Innovating

Edwin Land, a scientist and prolific inventor, explained his criteria for taking on a new project: "It needs to be a worthwhile project and it needs to be impossible." The first criterion is reasonable; the second is shocking. Land meant that the worthwhile project should also be one that pushes beyond conventional (or convenient) boundaries into new and innovative areas. This is at the heart of this Habit.

The three actions that make up this habit are characteristics of creative people. *Creating* implies the ability to generate an abundance of original ideas and to elaborate on them in detail. The capacity to generate new ideas is inherent in humans, but it needs to be developed. *Imagining* implies the ability to visualize and to think nonlinguistically. Athletes in both individual and team sports are frequently taught to visualize successful performance. *Innovating* implies the ability to find new ways to implement ideas, both old and new.

Responding With Wonderment and Awe

This Habit involves the capacity to find enjoyment within one's mind. It is the intellectual and emotional pleasure of finding beauty in a sunrise, a poem, or a piece of music. It is the intellectual surprise at finding something new and different or gaining some new insight or understanding. It is an intellectual and emotional reward for thinking about what we experience.

This Habit is an important stimulus for further thought. Seeing something that amazes us stimulates a curiosity about it, a sense of wondering about its origin, its meaning, and its causes. This Habit can be developed by seeking events that astonish and then concentrating thoughts on them. Every parent and teacher understands the sense of achievement they feel when their child's or student's face lights up. Sometimes it is a look of wonderment because they have never seen anything like that before, sometimes it is a look of joy because something has touched them deeply, and sometimes it is that amazing "aha" moment when suddenly it all makes sense. These moments can be fleeting, but they are powerful, and we need to seek them out.

Thinking About Thinking (Metacognition)

Chapter 3 was devoted to metacognition; in that chapter we defined metacognition as the conscious application of an individual's thinking to their own thought processes with the specific intention of understanding, monitoring, evaluating, and regulating those processes. It is thinking about one's thinking specifically in order to improve the efficiency of how we think. In fact, as pointed out in

Chapter 3, one of the elements of our thinking about our thinking is our behavior in support of what we are thinking. This behavior is embodied in all of the Habits of Mind.

This Habit is the foundation for all of the other Habits of Mind. The development of any Habit requires a mental recognition that it is being used and thoughtful reflection on how effective it is.

Taking Responsible Risks

You can't make an omelet without breaking eggs. Executing any plan of action is usually accompanied by the irreversible expenditure of some resources, and no plan is failsafe. When a person sets out on a specific course of action, he or she cannot be certain of the outcome. It is important to understand that any activity can have multiple possible outcomes. Anticipating various outcomes and evaluating their consequences is critical to any planning process. One can grow in this Habit first by focusing attention on anticipating risks when planning activities, then by assessing those risks and weighing their consequences against probable gain.

Most actions that aim at a worthwhile objective have risks associated with them. Intelligent persons understand those risks and their long- and short-term consequences before they act. They do not proceed blindly but with carefully reckoned assessment of the real risks they will face. In the home and in the school we need to create an environment in which learners feel safe enough to risk failure. Without taking risks, there is no growth. We learn a lot when we take risks, and we learn a lot from our failures. We learn how to be resilient and flexible and to look for other ways to do things. Some of our most intelligent young people are limited in their growth because we don't give them enough opportunities to take risks. A student who continually gets perfect scores on tests and assignments at school never has to take risks, because the work is never challenging enough. We do our learners a disservice when we do not make sure they have the opportunity to take risks and fail.

A successful learner understands the behaviors that will support thinking and learning and will grow in the ability to select them appropriately and apply them spontaneously. In other words they will become *habits* of mind, supporting metacognition and underpinning skillful, effective thinking. The task of the educator is to explicitly teach these behaviors by integrating them into the curriculum so that they will eventually become habits that are activated whenever problems need to be solved.

Summary

The 16 Habits of Mind are the behaviors of effective thinkers when they are faced with difficult problems. We are behaving metacognitively when we interrogate these behaviors, assess their effectiveness, and adjust them as necessary. There are various ways in which we can organize these 16 Habits; we have offered one suggestion. Some of the Habits seem related to personal traits, while others are more closely focused on the ways in which we acquire information, the particular thinking tools we are inclined to use, and the ways in which we respond personally to our thoughts. The teaching of these behaviors is best achieved by explicitly weaving them into every aspect of the curriculum.

THINKING DEEPER: DISCUSSION QUESTIONS

1. Most of us have either learned how to ride a bicycle or taught someone else to do so. Consider the process of learning this skill and identify the Habits of Mind that made it possible.

2. Do you understand your own strengths and weaknesses? Can you identify a Habit that you use most of the time and another that you feel you need to develop?

3. Which Habits might you want to focus on first with your own students? Why?

Endnotes

1. (Habits of Mind) The following websites contain information about the Habits of Mind:

The original website of Art Costa and Bena Kallick: http://www.instituteforhabitsofmind.com/

A site developed by James Anderson describing Habits of Mind in Australia: http://www.mindfulbydesign.com/

A teachers' network on Habits of Mind developed by James Anderson: http://www.habitsofmind.org/

5

The Wright Brothers

An Example of Skillful Thinking

We were lucky enough to grow up in an environment where there was always much encouragement to children to pursue intellectual interests; to investigate whatever aroused curiosity. In a different environment, our curiosity might have been nipped long before it could have borne fruit.

—Orville Wright

On December 17, 1903, the first flight of a heavier-than-air craft took place at Kitty Hawk, North Carolina. The aircraft was designed, built, and flown by two brothers from Dayton, Ohio; the flight ended a quest involving hundreds of scientists, engineers, and inventors from all over the world, many working with significant support from their government. Neither of the two brothers, Orville and Wilbur Wright, had a high school diploma. Yet, on that day they changed the world. The production and use of aircraft is today, over a century later, a multibillion dollar industry; it affects all aspects of our lives.

How could two young men, working alone, without formal training in science and engineering, breach the frontiers of aeronautical engineering to solve all of the difficult technical problems associated with flight? *Orville and Wilbur Wright knew how to think, they knew how to ask the right questions and to solve problems, they had an intellectual curiosity that drove them to attack an impossible problem, and they had confidence in their ability to succeed.*

The Wright brothers owned a bicycle shop in Dayton; aeronautical experts of their day would have given them a very small chance to succeed in a venture dominated by the intellectual giants of the field. They modestly attributed their success to their upbringing. Much later in his life Orville wrote the quotation appearing at the head of this chapter (Kelly, 1943).

We don't know exactly how Wilbur and Orville Wright thought, but we can make a reasonable conjecture based on the work of Arthur Costa and Bena Kallick described in the previous chapter (2000). Considering the Wright brothers' stunning accomplishment, it is interesting to reexamine their performance in light of these Habits of Mind. In the words of Peter Jakab, who wrote extensively about the Wright brothers' process of invention, "There were a number of specific personality traits, innate skills and particular research techniques present in the Wrights' approach that came together in a unique way and largely explain why these two men invented the airplane"(Jakab, 1990, p. xv).

In retrospect, we can see that the thoughtful behavior of the Wright brothers corresponds closely to the habits described in the previous chapter. So now let us examine how the Wright brothers exhibited the characteristics embodied in the 16 Habits of Mind.

Personal Traits

Persisting

The whole enterprise of first flight is evidence of the Wrights' persistence. They focused their efforts on one specific objective: to make an airplane that would fly. With that clear goal in mind, they set out to identify and solve the technical problems that stood in their way. Often a first attempt at solving a specific challenge was unsuccessful, but they persisted in finding different ways to approach it. For example, at one stage they needed to determine the best shape for the wing surface. To do this, they had to measure the effectiveness of various possible wing shapes, so they began a series of experiments for that purpose. Their first attempt was to modify a bicycle to carry a model wing shape through the air as fast as they could move the bicycle. This proved unreliable because the roads were too bumpy to extract accurate measurements, so they constructed a wind tunnel and forced air over a stationary wing model, which gave much better results. Eventually, they used kites and gliders to refine the design of their wings.

Throughout the enterprise, the Wright brothers had confidence in their ability to achieve their objective, even though, in the early stages, they could not clearly see the path to success. Persistence begins with a clear idea of one's objective—whether it is a grand goal like the Wrights' or a simple task that needs to be completed. Persistence then requires a willingness to try new ways to achieve the objective and the confidence in one's ability to get job done.

Managing Impulsivity

With a clearly defined goal, the Wrights focused directly on the steps required to reach it. Along the way they had to fabricate instruments to gather aerodynamic data, and then use this data to design the various components of the first aircraft, and finally test it thoroughly before the first manned flight. Throughout this process they did not waver from their goal. They were not distracted by interesting but unproductive sidetracks. The Wrights consciously focused only on the practical questions that would bring them closer to their airplane. As they worked on individual parts of the plane, they always kept the entire aircraft system in mind. At times, when they needed to think creatively, they allowed their minds to range freely over all possibilities. Managing impulsivity sometimes requires reining in free thought in order to focus on the task at hand and at other times letting thoughts run freely in order to foster the generation of new ideas.

Striving for Accuracy

Clearly, in an enterprise such as this there is little room for error. Not only did the Wrights need to work as accurately as possible, keeping the margins of error small, but they needed to fully understand the implications of any inaccuracy. They read the work of others to bring themselves to the frontiers of aeronautical science, but they also checked that information carefully before they would use it in their design. In several cases, they found errors in the open literature, which they corrected. They did not accept the conventional wisdom but tested all information against their own intuition and, when they felt it was necessary, by direct experiment. An important part of striving for accuracy is recognizing that knowledge is not absolute and that uncertainty accompanies the search for new knowledge. Consequently, uncertainty needs to be regularly assessed.

Finding Humor

On their way to first flight, the Wrights experienced many failures, which often ruined apparatus that had taken time and resources to prepare. Rather than accepting defeat, they consistently accepted these setbacks with a sense of humor. For example, in early tests at Kitty Hawk, their gliders would sometimes fall to earth with great force, burying their noses in the sand. The Wrights referred to these failed experiments as "well digging," and they listed well digging among their accomplishments. They labeled one particular sand dune that had intercepted many of their trial flights as the "Hill of the Wreck." Furthermore, life at Kitty Hawk was often harsh: cold, windy, and buggy. They accepted these hardships humorously, as a part of their quest. Humor helped to smooth out the rough patches in their enterprise.

Acquiring Information

Gathering Data Through All Senses

An important conception original to the Wrights' design of an aircraft was a flexible wing to control the flight path. This idea originated from the Wrights' observations of buzzards in flight; they noted how the birds altered the shape of their wings to adjust to changing winds. The actual mechanism of airplane wing warping was conceived by Wilbur as he absentmindedly twisted an empty bicycle inner tube box while chatting with a customer. These important insights came from simple activities unrelated to seeking a solution to a problem. Of course, the Wrights checked these concepts thoroughly. As experienced kite flyers, they used the sight, feel, and sound of their kites to help control them. Gathering data through all senses involves being constantly alert to new ideas and expecting them in unexpected circumstances.

Listening With Understanding and Empathy

The Wright brothers did not always agree on how to interpret their findings or how to proceed with their tasks. They had learned to resolve their differences as children when their parents encouraged each to listen carefully to the ideas of the other and to understand the other's viewpoint. These listening skills fostered the thoughtful and productive exchange of ideas between them.

Communication at the beginning of the 20th century was quite different than it is now. Working in Dayton, the Wrights did not have much chance to meet face-to-face with others working on developing aircraft. The main method of communicating was letter writing; they maintained an active communication with the Smithsonian Institution and with Octave Chanute, a respected expert with an international reputation in aeronautics. Eventually, it became clear to the Wrights that they were well ahead of Chanute in their understanding of how to construct an aircraft. Nevertheless, their communications with Chanute remained respectful and empathetic to his suggestions, even when they knew they could not work.

Questioning and Posing Problems

Faced with a complex objective, they divided their work into four major important questions: *lift*—how do we get the aircraft off the ground? *propulsion*—how do we move the aircraft forward through the air? *control*—how do we guide the craft's motion through the air? and *structure*—how do we build the airframe strong enough to support the machinery and pilot but light enough to get off the ground? These four questions provided an understanding of what needed to be done and outlined a systematic process for discovering the answers. Their progress in this project was guided by the curiosity nurtured in them as young lads. The intellectual curiosity fostered in Wilbur and Orville as children had blossomed into their ability to ask key questions, and asking the right questions led them to first flight.

Remaining Open to Continuous Learning

The knowledge that the Wrights brought to bear on problems they needed to solve included experience from toys they had played with as children (especially flying kites), their observations of the natural world, measurements they had made, and readings of the work of others. Their final conception of the aircraft evolved through a series of stages as they learned more and more about powered flight. This continuity of design resulted in a series of increasingly sophisticated gliders and powered machines that eventually led to the successful first flight. The curiosity nurtured in them as children led them to continue seeking new knowledge. It was the intellectual challenge of inventing the airplane as much as anything else that led them on. Remaining open to continuous learning is a manifestation of one's own curiosity.

Thinking Tools

Thinking Flexibly

The Wrights did not accept the conventional wisdom, which was to design an inherently stable aircraft. They recognized that the bicycle was unstable but with proper design it could be safely controlled. Eventually, as described before, they conceived of the warped wing for active wing control.

In implementing their conceptions of the aircraft, they made use of mental models to visualize the plane's performance. Their use of visualization and graphical representation is now recognized as an important element of learning and problem solving (Marzano, Pickering, & Pollock, 2001). They were able to move easily between abstract concepts and practical devices; combined with their use of visualization, this led to their ingenious and ultimately successful design.

Thinking and Communicating With Clarity and Precision

Even though the Wrights worked alone, they did communicate with others working on flying machines, primarily by mail. At various times they had specific needs to communicate with others. For example, they had originally planned to use a commercial engine for propulsion but, not finding a suitable one available, they designed their own. They needed to transmit their design clearly and precisely to an engine mechanic, who eventually built it. However, their primary communication was with each other, and this was based on the experience of years of working and playing together. After the first flight, they wrote clearly and accurately about what they had done, transferring their insights to the public domain.

Thinking Interdependently

As brothers who had grown up playing, studying, and working together, each came to know how the other thought. While they had few opportunities to interact directly with others on technical matters, they had a well-developed interdependence that allowed them to develop ideas in unison. They had a capacity for developing conceptual models of a problem that they could use to discuss the problem and that could then be transformed into practical hardware.

Applying Past Knowledge to New Situations

The brothers began business together with a printing shop, using a press that they developed together. They later opened a shop where they designed and built bicycles, the new rage in personal transport. Throughout their work on designing and building aircraft, they called upon the experience in their two previous enterprises. In particular, their knowledge of bicycles was invaluable. The knowledge they gained from the design of a safely controlled bicycle was used in the design of a safely controlled aircraft.

Personal Responses to Thought

Creating, Imagining, Innovating

Wilbur and Orville Wright invented a fundamentally new technology. They were not just the first persons to make an airplane fly; they also introduced and perfected several original design features essential to the success of the project. They were able to do this because of their ability to think creatively. One important aspect of this was their facility with nonverbal thought—visualizing using mental images and controlling those images in their "mind's eye." The importance of nonverbal thought in the creative thinking of inventors was noted by Ferguson (1977) many years after the Wrights. Recent research on the brain indicates that 90% of sensory input to the brain is visual; the brain responds differently to symbols and images than it does to linguistic input. The Wrights understood this early and incorporated visual thinking into their own thought processes.

Responding With Wonderment and Awe

One of the young Wright brothers' early toys was a helicopter powered by a rubber band. The toy was developed by Alphonse Pénaud, an early aeronautical pioneer. The boys were so impressed with the toy that they made several copies of it in various sizes. This response to a toy that interested them provides clear evidence of their curiosity and their ability to respond with wonderment and awe. They were also keen observers of nature, including birds; this led to their incorporation of the observation of buzzard's flight into plane design. They took pleasure in recreational activities, for example, kite flying, long before they decided to develop the airplane.

Thinking About Thinking (Metacognition)

The brothers talked together about their ideas and how they evolved.

As each new problem presented itself, the Wrights asked themselves the same basic set of questions: What information is needed to solve the problem? Where can it be found or what techniques or tools must be employed to obtain it? How can this information be successfully and practically incorporated into the design? (Jakab, 1990, p. 47)

In writing about their work they demonstrate a clear understanding of the evolution of the ideas used to arrive at their discoveries; they appreciated the interplay of ideas on the way to a final conception.

Taking Responsible Risks

Many aspects of the research leading up to a first flight were inherently dangerous. Test flights with untried gilders were not without significant risk. At least four airplane researchers ended their careers in fatal crashes. Recognizing the risk of first flight, Wilbur and Orville took time to learn how to control the aircraft and to practice the control to the point where they could anticipate the consequences of each movement of the pilot. The Wright's had the original idea to think of the pilot as a part of the plane. When it came time to attempt the first manned flight, they had come to understand the intricate process of controlling a powered aircraft.

The Habits of Mind form a framework with which to explore human behavior related to thoughts and their consequences. In this case, they provide a guide to understanding the thinking that lies behind the Wrights' remarkable achievement. Three attitudes are distributed through the Habits of Mind. The first is vision: the Wright brothers had a vision of just how an aircraft could fly, and this vision drove them to succeed. The second is intellectual curiosity, which drove them to seek new knowledge. The third is self-confidence; throughout the project, the Wright brothers knew they could succeed, and that confidence carried them through to first flight.

As teachers work with their students, a focus on the Habits of Mind provides a useful way of examining the complexities of human nature and achievement. In literature, the study of character can include a consideration of the kinds of Habits of Mind that cause the plot to twist and turn in the ways it does. What kinds of thinking might have averted the tragic conclusion to *Romeo and Juliet*? What kind of thinking impelled Santiago to continue his struggle with the marlin in Hemingway's "The Old Man and the Sea"? Just what is Chicken Little telling us about the need for skillful thinking when he exclaims, "The sky is falling"? In history, might the Second World War have been averted if only the key political players had thought more skillfully? How might the judicious use of certain Habits of Mind help us deal with the current arguments over climate change? What is it about their thinking that makes some people into heroes?

Parents can encourage their children to face the world and realize their dreams by encouraging the kinds of thinking that will move them forward, especially at times when the going seems tough and the distractions are powerful. When we are able to pinpoint what it is about their thinking that makes some people successful, we are then in a position to adjust our own thinking and learn from their examples. That is the power of metacognition.

Summary

The development by the Wright brothers of the first heavier-than-air craft happened because they had vision, intellectual curiosity, and self-confidence. Within this context, these two men also had the capacity to think metacognitively and to apply the Habits of Mind to their problem solving. Their story is a powerful demonstration of the value of the Habits of Mind, and we can help our students discover other examples of similar successes in history, literature, and the world around them.

THINKING DEEPER: DISCUSSION QUESTIONS

1. Consider someone you think of as successful, whom you admire. That person could be from any walk of life. What were the Habits of Mind that enabled that person to become successful?

6

The Language
of Thinking

*How can I know what I think
until I hear what I say?*

Thinking is the talking of the soul with itself.

—Plato

The task of learning skillful thinking is not the same for all children. The teaching of thinking finds fertile ground in some schools and struggles to make any impression in others. Why is this?

Language and Society

A good example of the relationship between language and learning comes from Pat's experience as a principal in the United States.

> I was the principal of an urban elementary school in a poor, predominantly African American neighborhood. On one occasion, I was called upon to intervene in an altercation in the hallway. The fifth-grade boys were at the "push and shove"

stage, and voices were raised. In one such incident, I calmed things down and then sought to uncover the cause of the problem. "He say 'yo momma'!" protested one of the boys. The rest of the students were eager to chime in with confirmations. One boy had tears in his eyes and was clearly very agitated. I was at a loss. I was an outsider in this community, a middle class, Australian principal in a poor, black American school. The children did not understand that I did not understand. They were unable to explain the layers of implied meaning wrapped up in these four words, and it took a conversation with a teacher for me to unpack and elaborate what the other children had understood immediately.

From the first day I walked into this school, I knew that there was something fundamentally different about the language used by the children. It was far more than vocabulary choice, accent, or even dialect. What I observed was a heavy reliance on gesture and facial expression—the tendency to roll the eyes was common and viewed by the local teachers as almost a cardinal sin. The student utterances were typically short and direct, and, when talking with each other, were very animated, loud, and involved a lot of physical contact, often friendly but also often assertive. In the classroom, it could be extremely difficult to get children to offer more than one- or two-word responses to questions. It seemed to me that these children saw language as largely a means of establishing social order and getting things done rather than a way of exploring the world and ideas. It was also very clear from the paucity of parent involvement and the low test scores that education was not progressing successfully in this community.

To what extent might this unsatisfactory state of affairs be directly related to the language development of the students? One of the most influential thinkers about education, Lev Vygotsky (Wells & Claxton, 2002) saw *the linguistic and cognitive development of children as growing out of social interactions.* He also regarded language development as dependent on those interactions and saw it as the driving force in intellectual development. If these students were either unable or unwilling to express their thoughts in elaborated, explicit language, how could we begin to help them become metacognitive learners? To take control of their own learning, they would need to become aware of their own thoughts, reflect on them, understand the strategies they had been pursuing, and adapt and develop them. "How can I know what I think until I hear what I say?" How could we teach these students to be skillful thinkers if they did not have the language needed to reflect on their thoughts?

In 1971 Basil Bernstein, an English sociolinguist, published his thoughts about the relationship between language and social class. He proposed that there are two "codes" of language, *restricted* and *elaborated.*

The restricted code is the sort of language used in situations in which there is a great deal of shared experience and understanding between the communicators, where meaning is hinted at, suggested, or implied, and where a rich support to meaning is provided by body language, gesture, tone of voice, and other forms of implied meaning. Logical relationships or arguments are not explained. There is a focus on the concrete and the here and now. Typically, this restricted code is used between family members, close friends, or members of professional groups, where much is understood without needing to be spelled out. Teachers engage in this kind of restricted code discourse in staff rooms. Doctors do the same with their medical colleagues. You need to be an insider to fully understand.

When using an elaborated code, nothing is left to intimation or suggestion; everything is spelled out. Communication is filled with detail, sentences are complete, words are chosen with accuracy, and meaning is accessible to anyone who is listening. There is a tendency to use abstract language. Principals frequently use this elaborated code when explaining the intricacies of curriculum or assessment to parents, and good doctors understand the need for this kind of language when explaining diseases and therapies to their patient. We are using this elaborated language in this book.

Bernstein went further than simply describing these two codes. He pointed out that children have language systems that are formed by the conditions and socialization processes within which they are raised. He suggested that there is a correlation between socioeconomic classes and linguistic codes, arguing that children from families of low socioeconomic status generally have access to the restricted code only, whereas children from middle-class families typically have access to both. Because the language of education favors an elaborated code, children from poverty are more likely to experience failure because they have not grown up in families and communities that helped them to become skilled users of this formal, elaborated code.

Ruby Payne's work in the United States (2003) has suggested similar connections between socioeconomic background and language use. Payne describes both the register and discourse patterns commonly used by students raised in different social classes. Children raised in poverty often suffer from a lack of vocabulary—the raw material of language—as well as limited repertoires for the use of language. Louisa Cook Moats tells us that first-grade "linguistically advantaged" students know approximately 20,000 words, whereas "linguistically disadvantaged" students know only about 5,000 (2001). Research has shown that this gap actually widens as students progress through school; learning is not a linear process, and so a vocabulary gap existing at the beginning of the first grade is wider at the end of the term.

Language for those raised in poverty, according to Payne, is "Casual register . . . about survival," middle-class language is "formal register . . . about negotiation," and the language of the wealthy classes is "formal register . . . about networking" (2003). Formal register is described very similarly to Bernstein's elaborated code, and the casual register is analogous to Bernstein's restricted code. Payne comes to the same conclusion as Bernstein: Students from poor communities typically do not have access to the formal or elaborated register.

These two researchers largely agree on the socialization and early learning reasons for these disparities. The social structures within which poor children grow up are not conducive to the development of formal, elaborated language. Poverty creates specific kinds of stresses for families raising young children. Some of the described characteristics of generational poverty include a survival orientation that limits thinking to the here and now, a focus on oral and informal language with high levels of nonverbal communication, and a strong tendency toward polarized thinking. The parent in poverty is subjected to pressures concerning survival. The single mother may need to hold down two or even three jobs in order to pay the rent, feed and clothe her family, and provide the material possessions that are deemed necessary within her community. She may not be predisposed to explaining her decisions when disciplining her children because she doesn't have the time or the energy. The child who wants to play with matches is told "No," and the parent's response to the inevitable "Why?" is either a simple "Because I said so" or a rap across the hand if the child hasn't put down the box of matches. There is no explanation of consequences and no reference to previous discussions or earlier experiences with fire. A harried young working single mother trailing two toddlers with a third youngster sitting in the shopping cart is not likely to give them the time to discuss and make choices about breakfast cereal.

Fewer children today spend their early years at home with a principal caregiver than was commonplace 50 years ago. Economic needs as well as personal aspirations mean that parents are often not with their child during the day. Instead, the child is either in a play-group, nursery, preschool, or some other form of day care. What almost all of these settings have in common is a greater ratio of children to adults than the traditional home settings of the past. Formal studies and our own observations and experiences of these settings reveal a necessary preoccupation with the management of groups and organizational issues. Language interactions with individuals seem to most typically involve the asking and answering of questions related to activities that are taking place. There simply isn't time during a busy day with a group of children to engage in the extended, interactive meaning-making conversations that aid the development of language and thought.

The child at home with a parent or home-based caregiver who is attentive to the need for these interactions will engage in repeated conversations like this:

Parent: Johnny, put the bowl in the cupboard please?

Child: Why?

Parent: So we can find it next time. Put it in that cupboard over there.

Child: I put it here. (indicating a different place)

Parent: No, put it in the cupboard with the other bowls, so they are all together.

Child: I put it here? (pointing to a different cupboard)

Parent: Are there any bowls in there?

Child: (looking in cupboard) Yes.

Parent: OK. See if it fits.

Child: Nope.

Parent: OK. So where will you put it?

Child: In there. (Indicating original cupboard)

What has the child learned here? He learned a lot about negotiation, about the need to plan for future actions, about grouping and organization, about spatial relationships, and about cooperation. All this learning was mediated through language, promoted thinking, and took time. "The most important factor in language development is how much a parent talks to the child after birth, the complexity of their vocabulary and how well they focus the child's attention" (Phillips, 2009). In his book *A User's Guide to the Brain*, John Ratey cites research on the rate at which children from different socioeconomic classes encounter words. Children of professional parents hear on average 2,100 words per hour, while working-class children hear about 1,200 words per hour, and the children of welfare parents hear only around 600 words per hour (2002).

How much of this intensive, responsive conversation can take place in a playgroup, a day care center, or nursery school, where the general adult-to-child ratio is somewhere between 10:1 and 15:1 at 3 years of age (National Child Care Information and Technical Assistance Center, 2008)? What parent could imagine interacting in this way with 10 or 15 three-year-olds, while there is another similar group of three-year-olds nearby with another adult?

We know that families living in generational poverty typically do not have the circumstances or opportunities to make this kind of optimal language development possible, but providing time for exploratory, responsive dialogue with the young child is fundamental to both the development of thought and language and to the child's understanding of the role of language in his life and in society.

Language, Thinking, and Metacognition

Recognizing this key interrelationship between language and thinking, we understand that the problems students from poverty are experiencing in the school system are not only about language but also about cognition and metacognition. The 16 Habits of Mind are the dispositions that successful people who know how to think skillfully make use of when confronted with problems for which the solution is not immediately apparent. But making use of these habits is a far more difficult and complex task for students from poverty.

When a child has been socialized in a community that has no real sense of future, where living is here and now, the focus is on survival and planning is minimal, the value of managing impulsivity may not be apparent. Payne states,

> People living in poverty need to be able to defend themselves physically, or they need someone to be their protector. Middle class uses space to deal with conflict and disagreement, i.e. they go to a different room and cool off; they purchase enough land so they are not encroached upon; they live in neighborhoods where people keep their distance. (2003, p. 37)

When a boy from generational poverty is standing in the cafeteria line and another boy cuts in, his respect among his peers diminishes if he doesn't defend his turf physically. It is not a part of his repertoire of social skills to manage his impulsivity, listen with empathy, and communicate with clarity to resolve this conflict.

Similarly, the habit of persistence grows out of a readiness to plan for the future and to understand the present difficulties or failures as steps toward future success. Children in generational poverty live in the present and may have what Reuven Feuerstein has described as an "episodic grasp of reality" wherein events are seen as temporally unconnected and the connections between what happens yesterday, today, and tomorrow are not made (Feuerstein, Rand, Hoffman, & Miller, 1980). Given this sort of cognitive predisposition, it becomes extraordinarily difficult for children from poverty to be persistent in school or to learn from past experiences.

The work of Rebecca Wheeler (Wheeler & Swords, 2006) focuses on the structure of language and grows out of a similar recognition of the catastrophic implications of language deprivation. Working with teachers in the classroom and analyzing the kinds of nonstandard features of the written language of African American students, Wheeler noted two things: There was consistency in the nonstandard features of student writing, and typically their writing did not respond to teacher corrections. Teachers were repeatedly correcting student work but seeing the same nonstandard features appearing time and time again. Her conclusion was that students were, in fact, operating with a different linguistic code, one that had its own set of rules—rules that were different from the rules of Standard English. The task for teachers was not to correct "mistakes" but to explicitly teach students how to switch codes. By showing students the need for a second linguistic code in the educational and formal context, and then by teaching them the rules of that code, teachers have been able to improve the academic acceptability of writing by African American students.

The issue is not that one code or register is somehow better than another. The linguistically deprived child is not the child who speaks in the familiar, casual register of the home, the playground, or the street. Language deprivation is the lack of different registers for different contexts and the inability to switch between codes as appropriate. The linguistically deprived child is the child who is unable to switch between codes. There is great value in restricted codes in appropriate contexts—we don't want to devalue the implicit language of families and we could view much poetry as an example of a highly restricted code—but we do need to acknowledge that the elaborated formal codes are the language of education.

Language and Metacognition

Vygotsky explored the cultural and social roots of language development and the ongoing interrelationship between thought and language (Vygotsky, 1986). He argued, among many other things, that language mediates thought and, in turn, thought can become more complex and sophisticated through the increasingly sophisticated use of language.

Metacognition is an essential skill for successful learning because it enables the learner to take control of the learning process by revealing his thought processes to himself, thereby enabling him to monitor his own understanding and refine his learning strategies. Only by the exercise of metacognition can students become independent learners, states the Committee on Developments in the Science of Learning and the Committee on Learning Research and Educational Practice in its report *How People Learn* (National Research Council, 2000). The ability to metacogitate is dependent on the ability to use an elaborated form of language. Without facility with abstract, carefully formed, and explicit language, the student will not be able to think about thinking at any level of sophistication. This is why we have made the cognition and behaviors explicit in our chapter explaining metacognition.

As our children develop greater facility with the written language, they have another essential tool of metacognition. The development of writing has enabled us to externalize and archive thought, providing us with a broad source of cognitive effort upon which to reflect. Some of this may be our own cognition, as when we write down what we think, but much of it is the cognition of others as we read the words they have written. Without the involvement of reading and writing, our metacognition is limited to the here and now or to what we can actively remember. By developing the ability to write our thoughts down, we increase both the breadth and the depth of metacognition because we are no longer limited by what we can actually recall. The child who grows up in an environment that both welcomes and encourages the written language is at a metacognitive advantage.

Rebecca Wheeler's work with language code switching was also teaching students about metacognition. Students were being given an opportunity to consciously reflect on their choice of language and to adapt and adjust according to context. This is metacognition. The very act of exploring their language, understanding their language choices, and adjusting their linguistic strategies was helping to develop a new level of cognitive flexibility. This kind of work, in which language and thinking progress together, certainly leads to improvements in academic achievement, but, perhaps most importantly, these students were also enriching their ability to use language as a tool of thinking. By sharpening the tool, they were creating new possibilities for more skillful thinking. They were developing their ability to think metacognitively.

It is essential that we make it possible for all our children to develop those Habits of Mind that will assist them to become effective thinkers, regardless of their origins in wealth or poverty. The future of any country as an innovative, economically powerful nation is dependent on our ability to produce a well-educated, creative, and productive generation of thinkers. India and China have populations that dwarf ours, and their current scientific and technological growth outstrips ours. We cannot afford the luxury of relying on any single stratum or group in society for our next generation of innovative thinkers. We need to draw expertise from all sectors of the population, male and female, rich and poor, and all ethnic groups. The pool within which we discover and educate the intellectual leaders of tomorrow must be as large as possible.

Understanding the Problem

What can we do to help children from poverty develop the dispositions and habits of mind of successful people? First, we must understand the nature of the problem. Uncovering the hidden rules and social structures of different economic groups is a first step to the development of effective strategies to overcome the impediments to skillful thinking. Educators must understand the relationship between experience, language, and thought.

A clear-minded understanding of the nature of educational institutions as they are at the moment is also essential. With the emphasis on accountability and a results-based approach to education, we have a system that places great value on test scores for individual students, teachers, schools, and school districts. Most of our testing programs assess student skills, concepts, and content knowledge. Curriculum and testing are closely linked, so we find that most schools are teaching concepts, skills, and content because they know that these are the things that will be tested. This risks neglecting the most fundamental levels of learning—the development of those habits of mind and the cognitive strategies that enable students to *process* concepts, skills, and content. Only then can effective learning and thinking take place. The existence and use of these habits and strategies is closely tied to language because behavior, language, and thinking are so intertwined.

What We Can Do

Any steps we take to improve student achievement by building cognitive strategies must include the building of vocabulary. Without the words, there is no language. Without extensive language, there will be no skillful thinking. Classrooms should be places where children are active talkers and writers. Teachers must plan carefully to introduce new vocabulary every day. For students to incorporate new vocabulary into their own usable lexicon, it needs to be related to past vocabulary, embedded in an experiential context, and be used regularly in student-engendered spoken and written language. The rote learning of new words and definitions will not do, because language acquires real meaning through experience.

Children from impoverished backgrounds typically will have limited opportunities to access the experiences that help deepen and broaden thought and language in ways that further the goals of education. Many of these children have never been outside their own communities. Their homes contain few books, and newspaper reading is not a feature of daily life. Children self-select television programs and typically will not choose to watch more informative programs or those that will encourage them to think. It is unlikely that there will be an adult with the time available to discuss television programs with the children. Unless the school arranges for these children to visit museums, art galleries, concerts, zoos, botanical gardens, and the like, they will probably never make them a part of their lives. Schools must take on the task of providing students with the experiences both within the school and outside of the school environment. These experiences provide the fertile soil for language and thought.

Time must be found to expand and deepen the experience-based language use of students. Ample opportunities for explicit modeling, extended discussion, and free and increasingly directed writing should be provided within each school day. We know enough about learning to accept that exploration is a precursor to understanding. We also know that while a small amount of appropriate stress might assist learning, too much will close learning down. If we want our students to explore language, take risks, and push the boundaries of what they can do, we must provide safety and time.

Build vocabulary whenever you can. As students talk about experiences or explore topics and concepts, write the key words they use on large sheets of paper that are displayed around the room. Remember to change these whenever the topics change.

In younger classrooms, vocabularies can be enhanced when spelling lists are created from the words the students need and want to use, and the class can revisit and build on these lists of words. Younger children can go on a "word walk" each morning in which they follow the teacher around the room, reading every word they can find on a particular wall. Older students can build word lists that develop word networks by the addition of synonyms, antonyms, homonyms, and similes. The connections between words can be illustrated by extending root words through the addition of suffixes and prefixes; for example, the root word *electric* is not difficult to spell, but problems can arise with *electricity* and *electrician* because in each word the second *c* has a different sound. If the connection is made to the root word, the problem is solved.

If we want our students to feel safe enough to explore their own thinking through their use of language, we need to be careful about how we structure our lessons and set our expectations. Consider the following experiment with a group of student teachers, which demonstrated the effects of pressure and assessment on the writing of students. A group of student teachers was asked to make a list of three or four topics that they felt strongly about. Each student was then asked to select one of the topics and to write about it for 10 minutes. They were told that no one but themselves would read the material and there would be no correction for spelling, grammar, or punctuation. During the writing time, each writer was left undisturbed; the teacher remaining seated at the front of the room.

Without further discussion, the students were then asked to take a second topic and a second piece of paper. They were told that this time the writing would be collected and would be corrected for spelling, grammar, and punctuation. They were told that some papers would be selected by the teacher for reading aloud to the group. During the 10-minute writing period, the teacher walked around the room commenting on student progress and using the words and phrases familiar to most teachers: "Come on George, you've hardly started. Others have got a paragraph down by now," "Well done," "Take care with your letter formation, Joey; I need to be able to read this," and so on.

The final step was to do a simple analysis of both pieces of writing. Students determined the average length of both sentences and words in each piece. It will come as no surprise that both the average length of sentences and of words in the first sample was significantly greater than in the second. The first passage was more complex linguistically and conceptually than the second. What made all the difference was the provision of time without the pressure of assessment and its concomitant fear of failure.

Thinking takes time—time for clarification, for rehearsing, for rephrasing, for exploration, and for thinking about our own thinking as we get better and better at it. Hand in hand with this must go time for the development of language. Classrooms must create time for dialogue. Teachers must learn how to listen and how to question in ways that lead children to keep on thinking rather than simply shoot off a "right answer."

Dialogue is at the heart of language development. Infants demonstrate a drive to share meaning with others, to use both social and cognitive intentionality as they engage with those around them, and to point to things and name them. They actively seek to become involved in dialogue—the intentional use of language between people. This social dialogue is the root of language, the interaction that vitalizes and nourishes its development.

Teachers can devise all sorts of activities that allow students access to their own thinking and the language that goes on in their heads as they carry out a task. Thinking out loud is a kind of dialogue with oneself that provides the opportunity for half-formed, fuzzy ideas to be made explicit. Ideas formulated into language are more accessible to ongoing metacognition.

Stump the Teacher is a thinking-out-loud activity in which students try to find a word that the teacher will be unable to spell correctly. As the teacher writes the word on the board, he explains his thinking for each decision about each letter as he writes it down. Let's take the word *philanthropic*, which the teacher has heard but not seen. The teacher's thinking aloud might go something like this:

> OK. The first letter could be either *f* or *ph*, because they both make the same sound.
>
> But the word has something to do with caring for others, and somewhere I have heard the Greek word *philos* meaning "love" or "caring," so I think I should begin with *ph*.
>
> The first syllable is easy now—*phil*—hmmm. One *l* or two?
>
> The rule says if the *l* is preceded by a short *i* sound and followed by a vowel, I should use a double *ll*. OK. But that looks wrong. I'll go with my gut and only put in one *l* and see what I think when it's done.

Second syllable is easy—*an*

Third syllable—easy too: *throp*

And finally *ic.*

Now back to the *l*—is it one or two? Let's look at each. Nope, two just looks wrong.

When one person's problem-solving strategies are explicitly expressed in elaborated language, others are given access to them and have the opportunity to build their own repertoire.

Similarly, the teacher can demonstrate how decisions might be made about the opening paragraph in a report or discursive essay. While writing on the board, the teacher verbalizes every decision, every change of mind, and every alteration, giving the students insight into an important aspect of essay writing. Something similar can be done in mathematics by having the teacher work out a problem on the board while making his or her internal thinking audible to the students. Of course, the next steps are even more important, when the students have the opportunity to make thinking language explicit.

We can also demonstrate to students the role of different languages in different situations. Remember, the linguistically deprived student is the one who has access to a limited range of different language forms. In mathematics, students can find different ways of representing a problem: writing it down numerically, writing it in connected sentences, drawing a diagram, creating a story about the problem, or using some concrete materials such as counters. The focus here is on showing that there are different "languages" we can use to express very similar things, and they all have their own strengths and weaknesses.

Translating formal language into informal and vice versa can be done both in role play and in written form. Students can write the same content in three different forms—one to their grandmother, one an e-mail to a best friend, and one as a text message. Rewriting a historical document in modern colloquial language gives students an opportunity to manipulate the content, examine the language of the content, become more aware of their own informal language, and develop their ability to use language strategically and with intention. A fascinating and extensive study of early childhood language development carried out by Gordon Wells and others at Bristol University showed that

the child who is treated as an interesting conversational partner and whose contributions are taken up and extended by his or her interlocutor is likely to gain greater confidence in his or her own ability to contribute to collaborative meaning making. (Wells, 2009, p. 14)

For those children who have grown up without the opportunities for the rich dialogue that nourishes language and thought, the school must step in. "Language has the power to shape our consciousness; and it does so for each human child, by providing the theory that he or she uses to interpret and manipulate their environment" (Halliday, 2003, p. 145).

It matters little if our children learn enough content to pass the tests if they are not also learning how to be more skillful, metacognitive thinkers. How can they explore their thoughts if they don't have the language to express them? How will they develop the adaptive expertise that enables them to transfer their learning from one context to another? We described in the preface the differences between the TIMSS and PISA international surveys of student achievement. It is significant that the TIMMS score for U.S. students is above the international average, whereas the PISA score is at or worryingly below the average. One of the most significant differences between these two tests is that TIMMS evaluates the taught curriculum, whereas PISA evaluates the ability of students to apply what they have been taught, to transfer their learning from one context to another.

Time, Time, Time

So, let us assume a school that encourages the broadening of experiences both within and outside the classroom's walls; a classroom rich in words; a classroom where children talk, read, and write; a classroom where every child has access to a dictionary and a thesaurus and uses them regularly; and where dialogue is seen as a central learning activity. In this classroom, children are given the time to focus their attention on ideas, to grapple with difficult problems out loud, and to struggle to find the best ways to express themselves. Only in such a classroom will children from poverty have the opportunity to develop the elaborated language and the cognitive strategies they need to process the concepts, skills, and content knowledge that are specified in the curriculum. In such a classroom, children will develop the ability to become skillful thinkers as they gradually learn how to exercise the Habits of Mind.

Of course, the problem is always one of time. If we provide the time for children to develop linguistic proficiency and we give space in the curriculum to teach the ability to think, how will we find the time to teach the content? It's a matter of priorities. To teach curriculum content to linguistically deprived students who are unable to think metacognitively and become thoughtful, independent learners is to waste a precious opportunity. Such students may well recall enough through drill and practice of routines to accomplish the short-term goals of passing tests, but they are unlikely to become lifelong creative learners, and what learning they have committed to memory for the tests will evaporate as they ride the bus home.

When teachers are under pressure to focus on mandated test preparation with specified content, often with an imposed curriculum and pacing guides, there is little time for the dialogue and exploratory, metacognitive development of language that makes the growth of ever more skillful thinking possible. Imagine a harried parent in the supermarket with her daughter:

Mother: Just stay beside the cart and be quiet.

Karen: Can I go find the stuff for dinner?

Mother: No.

Karen: Why?

Mother: Because.

Karen: Please!

Mother: Just be quiet, will you?

Just as this mother is pressured into a restricted conversation, so too will the teacher under pressure to get the current topic completed and move on to the next miss opportunities to use language and dialogue to explore, reflect, plan, and deepen thought.

If we take the time to develop the linguistic repertoires of students and teach them how to think skillfully, then they will have the foundations for learning any future curriculum content and the abilities to apply and transfer their learning into the personal, academic, and professional frameworks of their future lives. These are powerful long-term goals.

Reassessing Priorities

We must reassess the role of the early years in our schools and acknowledge that children coming from different backgrounds have different needs. The differentiation of instruction is a popular concept among teachers and administrators, but often its application is superficial. Some of our children will have a level of language that will enable them to uncover and explore their thinking, while others will not. If these latter children are not provided with explicitly designed opportunities to develop the language skills necessary for metacognition, they will not become independent learners. They may pass tests by drilling and rehearsing information and routines, but they will not become the creative, innovative, and flexible thinkers that our times require.

Summary

We use different kinds of language, or codes, in different situations. Linguistically deprived children are those who have a limited range of codes at their disposal. While generalizations can sometimes be misleading, there is considerable evidence to show that the stresses of life in families that struggle financially are such that there are insufficient time and resources to develop the broad vocabulary and elaborated code that makes metacognition possible. If we understand the nature of this problem, we can make opportunities in the school day to increase the experiences, vocabulary, and elaborated language skills of our students.

THINKING DEEPER: DISCUSSION QUESTIONS

1. Can you think about something without using words?

2. Make a list of some of the words that your students use that were not a part of your language when you were at school. How much do you understand of the meanings embedded in those words?

3. What do you know about the extent to which the students in your school or class have extended conversations with other family members?

4. Consider the physical environment of your classroom. Recall what is on the walls, the resources you have, the way the tables or desks are arranged, and the classroom rules you have established. To what extent do all these things reflect a belief in the importance of language, discourse, and literacy?

7

Creative Problem Solving

The significant problems we face cannot be solved at the same level of thinking we were at when we created them.

—Albert Einstein

Solving problems is one of the most complex human cognitive activities, and among the most important. Problems of all sorts confront us daily. They range from simple choices such as what to eat for dinner to complex issues such as how to respond to global economic and environmental crises. Solving complex problems is a higher-order thinking process requiring the metacognitive skills we discussed earlier—understanding, monitoring, evaluating, and regulating our cognitive tools. As such, problem solving is a skill that can be developed and that improves with practice. Metacognitive, creative problem solving involves the skillful use of proven techniques. This chapter is an exploration of how to develop this skill. The process of exploration of how we solve problems is an example of metacognition, because we are engaged in thinking about our own thinking—in particular, how we think when we solve problems.

Problem solving is such a common activity that it is hard to find a comprehensive definition that covers all of its aspects. Often it is described using other terms, such as *decision making, planning, calculating, understanding,* and *modeling.* One dictionary lists the following definition of the word *problem:*

> *1 a:* a question raised for inquiry, consideration, or solution; *b:* a proposition in mathematics or physics stating something to be done
>
> *2 a:* an intricate unsettled question; *b:* a source of perplexity, distress, or vexation; *c:* difficulty in understanding or accepting (*Merriam-Webster's Collegiate Dictionary,* 2005)

All of these definitions describe problems to be solved or resolved. We assume a broad definition of problem solving that embraces all of these ideas.

Perhaps the first attempt at describing problem solving in western culture comes from Pythagoras (571–500 BCE). He was a philosopher, mathematician, and mystic who established a community of scholars in southern Italy, then a part of the larger Greek empire. Most of the work of this community is attributed to him.

Pythagoras discovered that the pitch of harmonious tones bear simple integral relations to each other, so that there was an underlying mathematical pattern to the sensations of music. He extrapolated this observation to the belief that the external world we perceive could be understood in terms of mathematical principles. In simple terms, he believed that *what we perceive we can understand.* Pythagoras and his school developed a methodology for approaching this understanding that involves five steps: observation, abstraction, understanding, description, and verification. The detailed conception of the universe we have today is due in large measure to the first steps taken by this Pythagorean school of thought (Baggini & Stangroom, 2004; Kahn, 2001; Russell, 1945). We will adopt a slightly more modern procedure based on Pythagoras's conception.

A Procedure for Approaching Problems

In a classic book titled *How to Solve It,* mathematician George Polya introduced a four-step process for approaching problems. Polya's book originally appeared in 1945, but is so popular that it has been reprinted several times, most recently in 2004. While the intention of the book was to solve mathematics problems, we can adapt the process to apply to problems in general.

The four steps Polya introduced as a backbone for analyzing a problem are as follows:

1. Understand the problem

2. Devise a plan for solution

3. Carry out the plan

4. Examine the solution obtained

These four steps provide a vernacular for thinking about how to solve problems. As we have stressed elsewhere, when thinking about how we think, it is necessary to have a language and a structure to give voice to and to monitor our thoughts. So in addition to providing an approach to solving a problem, these four steps help us think about where we are along the way to reaching a solution. For example, we might explain to ourselves that we understand the problem well enough to make a clear statement of it, and we have devised the first few steps of a plan which we are just beginning to carry out.

Let's now look at what is involved in each of the steps. We do so in the spirit of helping you start out on a process that you will take over as your skill with it develops. This is analogous to teaching you how to swim so that you can practice until you become an expert.

Understanding the Problem

The first step in solving a problem is to make sure it is stated clearly and that all aspects of it are understood. This involves deciding both what information is available and what information needs to be determined, then stating the problem with any special conditions or constraints imposed on the solution.

Often it is helpful to use a nonlinguistic representation of the problem, such as a diagram or specific notation, a flow chart, or a bubble map, to illustrate the relationship among the various components of the problem. This right-brain activity brings other parts of the brain to bear on the problem and integrates both sides of the brain to work on the task.

The problem needs to be *well-posed*. The information available needs to be sufficient to determine a solution. Information must not be redundant or contradictory. It may be necessary to revise the statement of the problem until it is consistent and clear. When the problem is understood, you should be able to write out a problem statement in a few simple declarative sentences (not more than about five sentences). The interdependence of language and thinking means that when we begin to express a problem in explicit, carefully chosen words, we also clarify our own thinking and understanding of the problem.

Here is an example of a problem statement: Alan is usually a cooperative child. During this last week he has been quite disruptive and uncooperative. I need to discover what is going on in his life to cause this change in behavior. When posing a problem in this way, it is important to uncover where one problem ends and another begins. Clearly, as a teacher or as a parent, we would want to do something to turn Alan's behavior around, but the actions to be taken constitute a different problem and will need to be addressed in their own right. The problem under consideration at this stage is discovering what's going on in Alan's life to cause the behavior.

Devising a Plan

The second step is to make a plan for solving the problem. Try to find connections between what is known and what is unknown. If these connections cannot be found immediately, that is, if there are gaps or missing links between components of the problem, then determining these links or filling the gaps becomes part of the plan for a solution. A thinking map is a very helpful nonlinguistic tool that aids in visualizing the links and points out the gaps in knowledge that may need to be filled if the problem is to be fully understood. Thinking maps are described in chapters 9 and 12.

Be sure to access your prior knowledge as you work out a plan. Ask yourself if you have seen a similar problem before or know of a related problem. Look carefully at what is unknown in the problem, and try to recall how you have handled a similar unknown in different situations. Think about how others might have solved similar problems.

Frequently, the problems we face appear complex because they are unfamiliar to us; it often helps to make them more familiar. So, when you cannot solve the proposed problem, find some related and perhaps simpler problem that you can solve. Or maybe you could solve one part of the problem (divide and conquer). Try relaxing one of the constraints; for example, if there are budgetary limits, try to solve the problem with an unlimited budget, and then explore reducing the cost.

You need to check that the plan uses all of the relevant information available and that all of the constraints are satisfied. Some of the information you cited at the beginning of the process may not be important and can be ignored, but be sure that no important information is overlooked. As you review your thinking map, you may choose to strike out those elements that are not directly helpful or relevant. Similarly, if there are constraints on the solution—time limitations, for example—they should all be satisfied. Check that you have taken into account all essential ideas involved in the problem.

Often the steps in solving a problem are not all known in advance, but may appear as you proceed with the plan. In this case, it is important to choose the first few steps carefully, carry them out, and then reevaluate the plan. Be prepared to modify the plan as you make headway. Plans may be dynamic, and need to be flexible enough to take account of the unexpected.

Now back to Alan's teacher's problem. Her plan might be this:

> I will compare his behavior now with his behavior in the past and identify the specific changes. I will observe him carefully and see if I can discover any triggers to his unacceptable behavior. I will observe him when he is behaving well and see if I can identify the reasons. I will ask other teachers if they have observed changes in Alan's behavior recently. I will do some research on this kind of problem behavior in the library or online. Then I will telephone his parents and relate my observations to them. Based on what I find out here, I will plan future steps.

Remember that it is the awareness of and thinking about the problem-solving process as you execute your plan that helps you sharpen your skills.

Carrying Out the Plan

Check each step as you carry out your plan. Verify that each step been completed correctly. Try to prove that each step is correct. Monitor your progress carefully. Are you on track? Is your plan leading you to a solution?

Examining the Solution Obtained

Verify your result. Check that your result satisfies all of the conditions of the problem. Is your solution consistent with what you already know? Perhaps you can find another way to develop the solution.

Evaluate how well your plan worked in solving the given problem. Could you use your plan to solve a similar problem in the future? What changes would you consider to make the process more efficient?

Alan's teacher may gather the information she has gleaned from others and evaluate it. Her next step may then be to form a plan to help Alan understand and alter his behavior. Remember that the problem was to *understand* the behavior change, not to change the behavior. That is another problem and will need to be addressed next.

Polya's four steps provide a template for approaching problems. They give you a place to start and provide the language and structure for you to monitor your cognitive processes and improve them. There certainly are other approaches. Nobel Prize–winning economist Herbert Simon developed a technique for problem solving in a business context that he called *rational decision making* (Anzai & Simon, 1979). It focuses on issues vital in a business context, in which there are often many solutions to a problem and the solver must choose the best one. Simon's three steps are

1. Identify alternatives

2. Determine consequences

3. Compare all outcomes and efficiencies

and they provide a good complement to Polya's procedure if it leads to several solutions.

Role of the Subconscious in Problem Solving

When you are watching a movie mystery, your conscious mind is following the action on the screen, but your subconscious mind is working, too. When you suddenly get the idea that the clues are pointing to the victim's husband, you have received a hint from your subconscious mind, which has been reviewing the past action. Your conscious mind begins to check this new idea for consistency with the rest of what it knows. Even when the conscious mind is engaged in thoughtful activity, the subconscious mind is active.

Many people describe their experience of fretting over a problem for days, only to have a good idea for solving it strike them when they least expect it—"out of the blue," so to speak. A common occurrence for crossword puzzle enthusiasts is to struggle with the word for a particular clue and not be able to get it. If they then put the puzzle aside for a time, the word pops into mind when they return to the clue. Similarly, you may be in conversation when a word or a name evades you, but comes to you later (in the same conversation if you are lucky). These are examples of the subconscious mind coming to the aid of the conscious mind.

If the subconscious mind helps us serendipitously, is it possible to harness and control this ability? Unfortunately, we know too little of the subconscious to gain control of it, but many people report successfully tapping into it.

Here is a recipe for involving the subconscious mind in problem solving:

> Make a careful statement of the problem (as Polya suggests, in no more than five sentences). Read the statement thoughtfully just before you go to sleep and any other times when your conscious mind is otherwise unoccupied and can focus on it. Your subconscious mind can work on the problem, and if it reaches a possible solution, it will present it to your conscious mind at some time when the conscious mind is not occupied.

Mathematician Richard Hamming spoke to engineers and scientists at Bellcore (the former Bell Labs) in 1986. His talk, titled "You and Your Research," was intended to give the young researchers insight on how to conduct their individual research. At one point he discussed the role of the subconscious in solving problems:

> Well, we know very little about the subconscious; but one thing you are pretty well aware of is that your dreams also come out of your subconscious. And you're aware your dreams are, to a fair extent, a reworking of the experiences of the day. If you are deeply immersed and committed to a topic, day after day after day, your subconscious has nothing to do but work on your problem. And so you wake up one morning, or on some afternoon, and there's the answer. For those who don't get committed to their current problem, the subconscious goofs off on other things and doesn't produce the big result. So the way to manage yourself is that when you have a real important problem you don't let anything else get the center of your attention—you keep your thoughts on the problem. Keep your subconscious starved so it has to work on

your problem, so you can sleep peacefully and get the answer in the morning, free. (Hamming, 1986)

Dimensions of Problem Solving

It is useful to consider the variety and scope of problems we can face. Hatano distinguishes between two types of expertise used by problem solvers (Hatano & Inagaki, 1986). *Routine expertise* is characterized by a high degree of procedural efficiency in a specialty area. *Adaptive expertise* exhibits both the core efficiencies of routine experts and the willingness and ability to modify skills to fit new contexts and to articulate the concepts and principles underlying these skills.

Edward de Bono makes a similar distinction between two types of thinking (1994b). *Operancy thinking* involves the skills needed for doing things and is similar to routine expertise, while *design thinking*, involving the skills needed to think creatively and innovatively, is similar to adaptive expertise. "You can analyze the past, but you need to design the future," says de Bono.

This distinction, whether expressed as routine versus adaptive expertise or operancy versus design thinking, is important because it marks the distinction between solving problems using usual or familiar methods and attacking them with nonstandard, creative, innovative techniques. Techniques to enable a creative approach to lateral thinking, or out-of-the-box thinking, are discussed in subsequent paragraphs.

Problems within a given field need to be expressed in the language of that field. That language is often expressed in a restricted code, as discussed in the previous chapter. But the problem-solving techniques used in one field can be extended to use in another field. It is useful to study problems in all areas. For example, doing word problems in science or mathematics can help hone the skills of analyzing available information, and developing a plan of action while solving problems in business can help us to list and explore options and evaluate consequences of a particular course of action.

Lateral Thinking

Lateral thinking, a term introduced by Edward de Bono (1968), refers to a way of approaching problems that involves a change in the pattern of thinking away from the dominant paradigm to an alternative which may provide unexpected insights or solutions.

Often, when a problem arises, so does a method of solution (if, for example, the problem is increased traffic, the ordinary solution is to widen the road). The solution to which the mind turns naturally is called the *dominant paradigm*. Lateral thinking is an attempt to find an alternative solution that is more innovative or creative.

Joshua Klein gives an example in a video available on the TED (Technology, Entertainment, Design) website (Klein, 2008). In a cocktail party conversation, Klein was told about pesky crows populating a friend's backyard and causing a great mess. The dominant paradigm here involved killing the crows. Klein was interested in exploring different, more tolerant solutions, and eventually developed a "vending machine" for crows—they would pick up scraps of trash and deposit them into the vending machine and receive a bit of food as a reward. Thus, they were trained to pick up rubbish instead of leave it behind because they were rewarded. Useful crows that actually clean up messes might make them a valuable urban asset rather than an untidy pest.

Lateral thinking is nonlinear thinking; that is, it does not proceed in a prescribed series of steps but it cuts across the obvious pathways and makes links we may not usually make. It requires effort to leave the dominant path; we describe a series of tools, developed primarily by Edward de Bono, for enhancing alternative thinking. It is important to recognize that it is not the *newness* of ideas we seek; new ideas must have *value*, not just be different.

Three of these techniques are as follows:

- Introduce a random element into your thinking
- Introduce a provocative operation
- Change perception of a problem (repeatedly)

Introduce Randomness

Here is a recipe for introducing randomness into your thinking:

- Clearly express the problem (as suggested by Polya).
- Randomly select a noun representing a tangible object. (This could be tricky, but here is a website that generates random words: http://watchout4snakes.com/CreativityTools/Random Word/RandomWord.aspx)
- As an alternative, here is a simple technique for generating a random word from your favorite dictionary. The web page http://www.random.org/integers will generate random numbers

(based on random atmospheric noise). You should generate several five-digit random numbers between 0 and 99,999. Let the first three of these digits determine a page and the last two the entry. (If that does not work because the page number exceeds the dictionary pages, the entry number is too large, or the word is not a noun, choose another number until you find one that works.)

- Write down as many characteristics of the noun as you can.
- Think about each characteristic and try to connect it to your problem and how that might offer a different solution.

Provocative Operation

Propose an idea or viewpoint which may not be inherently correct or consistent but which advances the thinking about the problem. For example, you might try to *solve the reverse problem*. For example, if the problem is to reduce traffic congestion, you might consider ways to increase traffic, and reason as follows. To increase traffic congestion, we need more cars, which require more drivers. To find more drivers from a fixed population, we can reduce the age limit on drivers. Now, reverse this solution, and find that a strategy to reduce traffic is to increase the driver's age limit.

Alternatively, you can *challenge some element of the situation*. Ask why? (Should the United States adopt an isolationist foreign policy? Is a zero tolerance policy effective in curbing drug abuse? Should voting be compulsory?) You might make a statement that provokes thought and then analyze it.

Change Perception of a Problem

Another way to promote lateral thinking is to *change the way of looking at the problem.*

You may adopt a different point of view or a different person's perspective.

An important way to look at a problem differently is to use a graphic representation of it. The nonlinguistic nature of the new representation is a right-brain activity. Often a flowchart, bubble diagram, or matrix will expose relationships not evident in other ways. It frequently helps to pose a simpler version of the problem for consideration. Traffic congestion can be reduced by reducing the number of trucks on the road, so look for ways to reduce the number of trucks at rush hour. Or you may generalize the problem:

Instead of focusing on the problem of homelessness in your city, look at the problem in your state.

Lateral Thinking Tools

Edward de Bono has introduced two sets of tools to support lateral thinking. The objective of these tools is to make the intention to think clearly concrete, to help make the thinking explicit (1994b). The thinking tools described here are part of a program designed by de Bono called the Cognitive Research Trust (CoRT); more information about this program, which has been used by millions worldwide, can be found at http://www.edwarddebonofoundation.com

Six Thinking Hats

The hat one wears is a metaphor for adopting a particular point of view. While wearing a hat of a specific color, one assumes a particular attitude of inquiry. Each of the attitudes is represented by a different colored hat and is described below.

White Hat. With this thinking hat, you focus on the data available. Look at the information you have, and see what you can learn from it. Look for gaps in your knowledge, and either try to fill them or take account of them. This is where you analyze past trends and try to extrapolate from historical data. It's all about the acquisition of information.

Red Hat. Wearing the red hat, you look at the decision using intuition, gut reaction, and emotion. Also try to think how other people will react emotionally, and try to understand the intuitive responses of people who do not fully know your reasoning. This hat examines the human element, first impressions, emotions, and other people's points of view.

Black Hat. When using black hat thinking, we look at things pessimistically, cautiously, and defensively. We try to see why ideas and approaches might not work. This is important because it highlights the weak points in a plan or course of action. It allows you to eliminate them, alter your approach, or prepare contingency plans to counter problems that might arise. Black hat thinking helps to make your plans "tougher" and more resilient. It can also help you to spot fatal flaws and risks before you embark on a course of action. Black hat thinking is one of the real benefits of this technique, because many successful people get so used to thinking positively that often they cannot see problems in advance, leaving them underprepared for difficulties.

Yellow hat. The yellow hat helps you to think positively. It is the optimistic viewpoint that helps you to see all the benefits of the decision and the values in it, and spot the opportunities that arise from it. Yellow hat thinking helps you to keep going when everything looks gloomy and difficult.

Green Hat. The green hat stands for creativity. This is where you can develop creative solutions to a problem. It is a freewheeling way of thinking, in which there is little criticism of ideas. A whole range of creativity tools can help you here, including lateral thinking.

Blue Hat. The Blue Hat stands for process control. This is the hat worn by people chairing meetings. When running into difficulties because ideas are running dry, they may direct activity into green hat thinking. When contingency plans are needed, they will ask for black hat thinking, and so on. The leader wears a blue hat when there is a need to ensure that each hat gets adequate time and to keep to the agenda.

Attention-Directing Tools

The second group of tools is a set of concepts that focus the thinking on a particular aspect of the problem (de Bono, 1994b). They help us retain focus. Each of the concepts has an acronym for easy recall, and it can be used to describe the activity behind the concept. The acronyms provide the language to use in discussing the thinking activity. For example, a teacher wishing to have students engage in an analysis of Truman's decision to use the atomic bomb at the end of World War II might say "Let's do a PMI on that decision" or "Let's examine the APC of the situation." Below we give a brief description of seven attention-directing tools. The different tools are not completely independent but overlap somewhat.

PMI (Plus, Minus, and Interesting). An evaluation of an idea for its positive and negative values and those neutral aspects which may also be interesting.

CAF (Consider All Factors). A check to see that all factors are considered and all issues are addressed.

APC (Alternatives, Possibilities, or Choices). An exploration of alternatives to a given course of action or a listing of various choices which may be made.

C & S (Consequences and Sequel). An attempt to anticipate all the consequences of a course of action and to predict what may result.

FIP (Focus on Priorities). After PMI, CAF, APC, and C & S thinking, one orders one's priorities to set objectives (AGO).

AGO (Aims, Goals, and Objectives). Clarifying the objectives of the thinking.

OPV (Other People's Views). Examine how others might view the action taken as a result of the thinking.

Once again we can see the value of having explicit words (or acronyms) to make the process of thinking explicit. The language can be used to direct thinking and to give us a vocabulary that makes thinking about our thinking, metacognition, accessible.

In All This Analysis, Don't Neglect the Human Element

The statement of a problem frequently emphasizes its analytical character; posing problems is essentially a left brain activity. The human element of the problem is then ignored. To compensate for this it is important to reconsider or reevaluate the problem and its solution in human terms.

Here is a simple example (drawn from a puzzle presented on the radio program *Car Talk* on American National Public Radio).

The puzzle. Two travelers and a vagabond meet at an oasis at the end of a day's journey. All three are tired and hungry. One traveler has five loaves of bread, and the other has three loaves. They agree to share the loaves equally and do so. After the meal, the vagabond draws out his purse, which contains eight coins; he gives five to the traveler who contributed five loaves and the remaining three to the other traveler.

During the night, the vagabond thinks that he has made a mistake and distributed his coins unfairly and in the morning raises this question to his two companions. They all agree and redistribute the coins. How were the coins redistributed?

The solution. As posed, this is a mathematical problem. The details of the solution are unimportant, but a fair distribution can be calculated; it requires the man with five loaves be given seven coins and the man with three loaves be given one coin—a bit of a counterintuitive surprise. An easy way to reckon the solution is to consider each loaf as divided into thirds, with each man receiving one piece of each of the eight loaves. The man with five loaves (15 thirds) eats eight thirds of a loaf and contributes seven thirds of a loaf to the group; the man with three loaves (9 thirds) eats eight thirds and contributes one third. Hence the adjusted distribution.

A postsolution reflection. So much for the left-brain portion of the puzzle. The fact remains that as the three men part the next day one has seven coins, one has one coin, and the vagabond has no coins. Their prospects for the next night's meal are quite uneven. Taking into account the right-brain side of the situation, a second redistribution of the coins would be required. The original puzzle was designed for an easy solution to the mathematical problem, but there is not such an easy or unique solution to the human problem.

Solving problems creatively and effectively is complex, and it is most likely to occur when we are in control of our thinking. When we have the ability to select from a range of tools, when we can monitor their effectiveness and evaluate and adjust our use of them, then we are thinking metacognitively. Metacognitive thinkers are more successful learners and more effective problem solvers.

Summary

One of the most common and complex intellectual activities we engage in is problem solving. Many attempts have been made to describe the process; we have explored one of these, namely that of George Polya. The subconscious may be largely inaccessible to us, but we can draw on its resources to help us solve problems. We have also explored the ways in which various techniques of lateral thinking can help us solve problems. Whatever tools or procedures we use to deal with the conundrums and problems of daily life, we will be more effective if we understand what we are doing and use that metacognitive understanding to select and adapt our approaches.

8

Knowledge Networks

The Organization of Knowledge
to Facilitate Metacognition

I read somewhere that everybody on this planet is separated by only six other people. Six degrees of separation between us and everyone else on this planet.

—John Guare, *Six Degrees of Separation*

We recently had the joyful experience of spending a month-long holiday with four of the youngest members of our extended family, their ages ranging from four weeks to three years. As we interacted with them, we saw the dynamic changes in the way their brains organize experiences and information over these first dramatic years of life.

When we first encountered Charlotte, the youngest, she appeared to be immersed in a sea of unrelated and random stimuli and sensations. If a face drifted into her field of vision, she would sometimes focus on it for a moment, but more often she would seem to be gazing off into the distance. Only three weeks later, things had changed dramatically. Charlotte would turn her head, seek out specific faces, stay focused on them, and respond with a smile. Her excitement grew when she saw her mother approaching her, and the smile would widen. If she was hungry, her agitation would increase to an almost frantic level as she noticed the minute preparations by her mother for feeding time. What had happened in those three weeks? Charlotte's brain had begun to make connections. Her ability to predict was growing as she linked past experiences together with what was going on in the present. You could almost hear the synapses sparking as new pathways were being continually created at an amazing rate.

Charlotte's four-month-old cousin Bridget was intensely interested in the people around her. She was able to anticipate a tickle because her brain had been there before, mapped the experience, and knew what to expect. Her brain had also created links between the people in her world and the things they did, so she was able to predict that a tickle was more likely from her daddy than from a stranger. In fact, if a stranger were to take the liberty of trying to tickle her, the lack of a clear neurological network based on previous experiences with that person would make her anxious and uncertain.

One-year-old Taj was immersed in the amazingly complex task of embedding language into the increasingly complex neurological networks in his brain. The question "Where is your hammer, Taj?" activated multiple pathways as he made the connections in his brain between his understandings of the intonation of a question, the meaning of the word *where,* his growing sense of person and ownership—it was *his* hammer—and his experience, from his first hours of life, that language is an interactive process, linking him with the others in his world. Within Taj's brain there was a constant process of synaptic linking as new experiences, new sensations, and new words were incorporated into his growing network of thought.

Three-year-old Abbie's brain is an intricately complex entity. She has organized three years' worth of sensation and information into a network that can incorporate and integrate each new experience into itself. She makes sense of the world because she has a brain that is flexible enough to change the connections, to create new pathways, and to integrate the new with the old.

She can plan, understand the difference between yesterday and tomorrow, and launch herself into every new experience because she has a brain that is plastic, integrated, and constantly changing to accommodate the new into the old.

What we saw in these four children was a process that does not stop at any specific age. It continues throughout life, with bursts of more frenetic energy at some times than others. We will never again match the sheer quantity and speed with which the young brain makes new connections, but our brains are networks that continue to grow and change throughout our lives as long as we provide them with the new experiences they need in order to thrive.

As we have discussed in Chapter 2, a well-established tenet of cognitive science is that experts organize their knowledge differently from novices. This was demonstrated in the early work of de Groot comparing the ease with which expert chess players could recognize and remember the configuration of pieces in midgame compared to less experienced players (de Groot, 1965). Subsequent studies of experts in different fields are described in *How People Learn* (National Research Council, 2000).

Newborn Charlotte is very much a novice and Abbie has developed considerable expertise. In large measure, successful teaching transforms students from novices to experts. At the beginning of the school year a student enters the classroom as a "novice" third grader and is expected to leave it at the end of the year as an "expert" third grader prepared to begin the next year as a "novice" fourth grader. We anticipate that the novice five-year-old reader will have developed considerable expertise by the time he leaves primary school. What is involved in this transformation? Certainly it involves the acquisition of knowledge, but more than that, the knowledge must be organized into a conceptual framework that allows it to be easily transferred to new and different situations. We want our rising fourth graders to have a level of expertise that allows them to use their knowledge in situations different from those in which it was learned.

The U. S. National Academy of Sciences report *How People Learn* describes an emerging understanding that effective learning requires an individual's introspection—a metacognition. One focus of this metacognition is on the organization of newly acquired knowledge. One of the three principle findings of this report encourages teachers to help their students "(a) have a deep foundation of factual knowledge, (b) understand facts and ideas in a context of a conceptual framework, and (c) organize their knowledge in ways that facilitate retrieval and application" (National Research Council, 1999, p. 12).

This implies that each learner must make a conscious effort to organize the information learned in a flexible enough way that it can be used in new or different circumstances. Without this organization, knowledge remains isolated and inert. Without effort by students to consciously organize the information they are learning, it becomes "episodic rote learning and memorization" (Costa & Kallick, 2008).

Beyond the most basic levels, the ability to organize knowledge is not an innate characteristic of humans; it must be learned. Some individuals may organize their knowledge in an unsystematic manner, but by using our recent understanding of how people learn, this process can be made more organized and effective and can be extended to all students. Teachers who can help their students with this organization will increase the efficiency of their learning and thinking.

Teachers have the knowledge that they expect to transmit to their students embedded within their own conceptual framework—their own personal mental construct. They can impart the knowledge they have, but they cannot transfer the construct in which that knowledge resides. A mental construct is personal and depends on experience, the state of one's mind when the knowledge was acquired and each time it was used. Even the meanings of the words we use are influenced by our differing experiences and the context within which the word is used. If you consider the word *cat*, each reader will have had a slightly (or significantly) different mental image. For some, it may be a well-remembered and much-loved childhood pet, for others a screeching, unpleasant animal that leaves fur all over the furniture; for some it's tabby and short-coated, for others a white puffball of a Persian. An engineer may even think first of a vehicle with a caterpillar tread. Think of the word *pretty*. Now consider the word *ugly*. See how both words change their meanings within a different construction when we say something was "pretty ugly." So how can we help our students create their own constructs? The purpose of this chapter is to shed some light on this question by proposing a model for knowledge organization based on recent results in network science. This model will provide a generalized setting within which a mental construct can be discussed.

The major difficulty in helping students monitor and evaluate their thinking is that each child's mind is accessible only to that child. Science can study an individual's brain, locating where different mental activities are activated, but science cannot delve into an individual's mind (Damasio, 1999). Consequently, we cannot determine how knowledge is stored in someone else's mind. It would help if we had some model of the possible ways that a person could organize knowledge in their mind.

The organization of information is an old question. Over 250 years ago Diderot and d'Alembert had considered how human knowledge can be organized and how that might reflect on the way knowledge is organized in the human brain (Diderot & d'Alembert, 1751/2011). The result was a hierarchical structure called the Tree of Knowledge, which has been added to from time to time. This structure was the basis on which Diderot and d'Alembert organized one of the first major encyclopedias. That early work has been revisited recently because it bears on how one might construct a knowledge network using hypertext in Internet sites like Wikipedia (Rockwell 1999). While it is useful to consider that work as an example of a network structure for knowledge external to a human brain, we are striving to understand the network construct within an individual mind.

We will introduce a simple model of the different ways that knowledge can be organized in a human's mind. It will illustrate the transformation from expert to novice we seek to effect in students. The model is based on what we have learned recently about the science of networks. While this model lacks the rigor of a fully developed scientific theory, it does provide insight into the possible stages of development of the mind as a storehouse of knowledge and can be used to inform teachers of the organizational processes going on in their students' minds.

The Emergence of a Science of Networks

A new area of scientific inquiry blossomed during the last decade of the 20th century. It focused on the study of networks and grew out of our need to understand the many complex networks that are vital to our well-being. Operating in the background of our busy, complicated lives are many complex networks responsible for the delivery of the goods and services we require, networks that provide for our food, water, power, communications, and so forth. When these networks fail, the consequences can be dire, as they were in the spectacular power outages of the 1990s and in the aftermath of catastrophic natural disasters like Hurricane Katrina. In addition, we have seen new networks emerge with mobile phones and the Internet, and we have come to a much better understanding of some long-existing networks such as the neurological networks in living organisms and the human genome. This new science has been applied to understand the behavior of networks for communication, distribution of resources, epidemics, management in organizations and, most famously, the Internet. There are two popular books describing network science, written by important contributors to the field (Barabási, 2002; Watts, 2003) as well as a comprehensive technical review paper (Albert & Barabási, 2001).

One of the most familiar results in the field of social networks comes from the work of psychologist Stanley Milgram, who sought to understand the connectivity of human social interactions (Travers & Milgram, 1969). He performed several experiments in which individuals in one community (in Kansas) endeavored to make contact with a remote target individual (in Massachusetts) using the social network of their friends and their friends' friends. The resulting notion of "six degrees of separation" implies that an individual in a particular population can contact another individual through a directed chain of, on average, six contacts. This idea, that we live in a "small world," has entered the popular culture through a play by John Guare, *Six Degrees of Separation*, in which a principal character, Ouisa Kittredge, says, "Everyone is a new door opening into other worlds. Six degrees of separation between us and everyone else on this planet. But, to find the right six people. . . ." The play was made into a movie (a good one— 93% on Rotten Tomatoes); there was also a short-lived TV series by the same name and exploring roughly the same idea.

So what is a network? Here is a simple example. If you have a modern mobile telephone equipped with a directory then you are connected to each of your entries; when you push a button on your phone, it connects to another phone. Each of those entries has its own directory connecting them to another set of telephones. And so on. So with your phone at the center, there are series of interconnections that extend far beyond you.

In general, a network is a collection of objects, called *nodes,* connected in pairs by *links.* The objects, or nodes, could be anything, telephone numbers as in the example above or neurons, or electrical power stations. The objects are linked by specified connection, being in a directory in the previous example, or by synapses between two neurons or cables between power stations. Figure 8.1 shows a network; nodes are represented by dots and links by lines connecting the dots. The network grows in complexity from left to right. In some cases nodes stand alone—not connected to any other node. In other cases, only two or three nodes are connected. At the extreme right there are a large number of nodes, interconnected in a complex way.

One of the easiest networks to visualize is the social network of your friends. You and each of your friends are nodes connected by links representing your friendship. Your node is connected to the nodes that are each of your friends; each of these nodes (friends) is connected to their friends, some but not all of whom are also your friends. As the network expands to more and more layers of friends, it comes to cover the globe. The surprising result of Milgram was that, despite the wide range and apparent complexity of a social network of friends, it is still possible to establish contact between two individuals with relatively few intermediaries (about six).

Despite the wide range of differences among networks and their varying degrees of complexity, there are a few characteristic properties which help to describe their general structure. The details of these characteristics are not important here, but are discussed in our earlier work (Buoncristiani & Buoncristiani, 2007). A remarkable result from

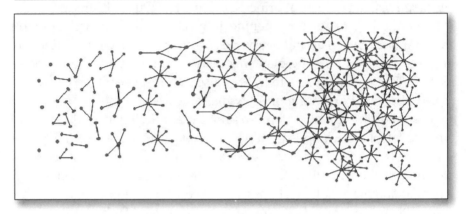

| Figure 8.1 | A network is a collection of objects called nodes that are connected by links. In this diagram each point represents an individual node in the network and each line represents a link. The network shown grows more complex from left to right. |

Source: Adapted from http://www.orgnet.com/prevent.html.

modern network science is that despite the fact that networks may be very different, they share the same simple organizing principles. Because these organizing principles hold for all networks so far studied, we can conjecture that they also exist for a human's network of knowledge.

There are three different kinds of networks, each at a higher degree of sophistication and organization. It is important to recognize these three network types because, as we will show later, they represent different ways that knowledge can be organized in our brain.

The first is a *random network;* as the name implies, the nodes are connected at random. Imagine a collection of nodes represented by dots as in Figure 8.1. The nodes or dots are not as yet connected. If connections between nodes are made in a haphazard manner, the result is a random network. It is a network with no regular structure.

The next kind of network recognizes that real networks are not entirely random but have an element of order. When you think of the collection of your friends, some you have developed because of the structure of your life (where you live, where you work, where you go to church) and some because of individual choices that you make (you play bridge, your hobby is photography, and you volunteer at the school library). These two elements (order and randomness) of your immediate social network, called *structure* and *agency* by sociologists, are responsible for the uniqueness of your friends and ultimately for the global connectivity of our world. Researchers have developed a mathematical model that allows for the systematic study of networks that have a combination of order and randomness (structure and agency). These so-called *small-world networks* have characteristics common to a large number of very different real networks.

The third type of network was discovered by examining the inter-connectivity of the Internet. A computer was programmed to explore all of the links associated with a specific web page, then all of the web pages it was linked to, and so forth. It mapped the network of pages it traversed as it crawled through the Internet. This task was far too tedious for a human but ideal for a computer. Examining the network obtained in this way showed a preference for a few nodes to have a very large number of links and a preference for new links to be made to these hubs (think of sites like Google, Yahoo, or Wikipedia). This preferential attachment is sometimes compared to the idea that "the rich get richer"; the more money you have, the more money you get, and so the more links a web page has, the more it is likely to get. Figure 8.2 shows a typical network with preferential attachment.

Figure 8.2	This figure shows a typical network with preferential attachment. In the figure, the hub nodes are shown as larger, their size proportional to the number of links. In a network with this sort of "preferential attachment," there are a large number of nodes with a few links and a few nodes with a large number of links.

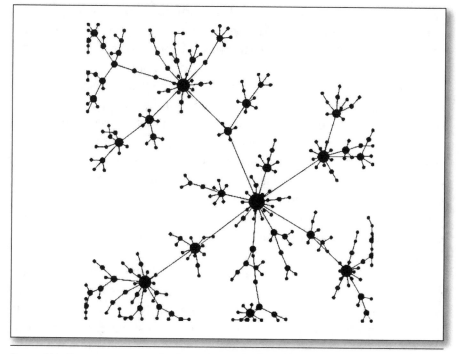

Source: This figure was generated using software developed by Uri Wilensky of Northwestern University and is incorporated in NetLogo: http://ccl.northwestern.edu/netlogo/models/.

In the figure, the hub nodes are shown as larger. In a network with this sort of preferential attachment, there are a large number of nodes with a few links and a few nodes with a large number of links. This type of network is called *scale-free*.

The technical details of network science are not so important here. What is important is that there is a hierarchy of three increasingly sophisticated networks—a random network, a small-world network, and a scale-free network, and these can be used to model the increasing sophistication of knowledge networks. We describe this hierarchy below as we develop a model for knowledge organization.

The most impressive result of this new science is that dramatically different types of networks exhibit common properties. It is our premise here that it is reasonable to consider an individual's mental construct for knowledge to be a network and that consequently it shares these properties. This understanding is useful to the extent that it can elucidate the organization of knowledge in the student's mind.

A Model of Knowledge Acquisition

We can think of the organization of one's knowledge as a network. Each bit of knowledge in the brain can be represented as a node in a network, and the connection among individual bits of knowledge can be represented by links. The resulting pattern of nodes and links forms a network—the network of an individual's knowledge, their personal mental construct. The manner in which information is organized in a person's brain, the structure of their knowledge network, determines the ease of accessing that information.

Some students treat each learning experience as an isolated event that is disconnected from their other knowledge. They are unable to describe how they learn. They do not question the processes by which they learn. Their learning is episodic, rote memorization. The knowledge they acquire is acquired for a specific purpose, a test, an essay, or a project and is not easily transferred to different situations. Consequently, when confronted with situations that confuse them, they have no resources to use to resolve the confusion. Their knowledge organization is, like the network in the middle of Figure 8.1, loosely connected.

One might know, for example, that the Battle of Hastings took place in 1066. A student might know that fact because his teacher told him that dates would be on the test, so he dutifully recorded it in his notebook and then reviewed it just before the test. After the final test, that information is effectively lost. Another student may be genuinely interested in English history and the succession of British kings. To that student, recalling the date of the battle causes a series of related ideas to flow to his consciousness. Hastings was the last time England was conquered by a foreign power. This insight requires knowledge of British history subsequent to Hastings. Furthermore, the battle stemmed from disputes over the succession to the English throne. This understanding requires knowledge of the previous history of Britain and the role of monarchy. The first student learned an isolated fact, while the second student found a context for his knowledge and placed this new piece of information within that knowledge network.

The knowledge network of any two individuals can be expected to be as different as their fingerprints. But, just as there are common characteristics for fingerprint features, there should be some set of common organizing principles governing how knowledge networks are formed. If we can understand these principles, we may be better able to guide the evolution of the mind's acquisition and organization of new knowledge. Indeed, this is the imperative of the primary findings of *How People Learn*.

The following is a hypothetical scenario of such an evolution, based on the nascent science of networks. It provides a tantalizing and plausible story for how knowledge grows within the mind. It illustrates the unsatisfactory nature of simple episodic organizational schemes and reinforces the need for personal effort in learning to achieve sophisticated understanding.

When an infant begins to learn, he or she is flooded with sense data; each new bit of information appears to be the same as every other bit, since there is no basis for discriminating between them. Since there is no discrimination among the bits, they are initially linked at random. The organization of early knowledge is a random network. It is featureless, with no structure to the information it contains. Something similar occurs when an adult begins to learn a completely new subject.

As more information becomes lodged in children's minds, the network configuration changes, and connections between bits of information become recognized and linked purposefully. One of the first bits of organized knowledge that an infant would construct is the persistence of mother. Each sight, sound, touch, taste, and smell associated with a mother's care is collected and connected until the child becomes aware that these sensations are linked to the same entity. Slowly this entity would gain constancy; the child would know there is a mother even if she was out of sight. Eventually the child would recognize other entities: father, siblings, and other friends and relatives. As the child grows, he or she would encounter other people, such as playmates or teachers, and be able to recognize each of them and their relation to people already known. This organization of information transforms a random network to a small-world network. Order begins to emerge from randomness. As more connections are discovered between bits of information, they begin to cluster. In a small-world network, there are clusters of knowledge, but also a few nodes in each cluster have long-range links, a remnant of the random network stage. These long-range links provide a connection among clusters.

This small-world knowledge network is characteristic of the novice learner. With no effort or guidance to organize new information, learning at this level tends to be largely episodic rote memorization.

When and if the learner begins to think about *how* the information she is receiving is organized, her knowledge network changes in a more profound way. The attachment of links begins to prefer those nodes which have already established more links. These preferred nodes, called *hubs*, form the centers about which information is organized. This organization forms a scale-free network. The chief characteristic of this stage is the appearance of hubs—centers about which knowledge is arranged without any bounds. The child who has first learned about mother, then about other people, may reflect on this knowledge and come to understand the more abstract concept of an *individual*. Individuals may be classified by their relationships to the child— these are my relatives, these are my friends, these are people I meet on the way to the market. The child may be able to think about individuals not yet met or anticipate meeting new people and being able to classify them in some fashion.

Thus, the evolution of the organization of knowledge can be seen to pass through three stages. In early learning, knowledge is organized at random, and the landscape is featureless. Later, as connections among the pieces of information are discovered, some bits of information begin to cluster, while other bits still retain a random element. Finally, the sophisticated learner begins to organize information around hubs.

It turns out that there is a dramatic technical difference between these three levels of network organization. The connectivity in the random and small-world networks is limited; in a given network, the number of links to any one node is limited. In the context of a knowledge network, that means a limitation on the connectivity among concepts. On the other hand, in a scale-free network there is no limit to the number of links to nodes. Thus some hubs can have an unlimited number of links, and the resulting network has no limit on its complexity imposed by the network structure. There certainly are limits on the complexity of a knowledge network imposed by the brain itself. This justifies thinking of the scale-free network as a network of the sophisticated knower.

Table 8.1   Development of the Knowledge Network

Early Learning	Novice Learning	Expert Learning
Random Network	Small-World Network	Scale-Free Network
Structureless	Clusters	Hubs
Bounded range	Bounded Range	Unbounded Range

Implications for Classroom Practice

We have introduced an idea about how knowledge can be organized in an individual's mind in three stages of increasing complexity. The idea is useful in thinking about how people learn, and may be useful for teachers who seek to help their students organize their new knowledge into a conceptual framework. There remains work to be done to validate this idea and to study the process by which a knowledge network develops, but experience tells us that it is a useful model.

The idea that a network structure describes the organization of knowledge in a person's mind allows us to discuss the process of learning for understanding. The language of network science can be used to clarify the process of flexible learning and provide guidance to teachers as they seek to implement the most effective classroom strategies.

This simple view of the evolution of an individual's organization of knowledge suggests a strategy for teachers. In aiding students to move from the early to the middle stage, teachers should assist students in recognizing connections among bits of information they are learning. In assisting the transition to sophisticated learning, teachers need to help students identify hubs of knowledge and fit what they are learning into these hubs. This description of the transition in stages from an early learner to a sophisticated learner could also apply when a sophisticated learner takes on a new subject. These hubs may not correspond with the disciplines taught in our schools.

A less sophisticated network may only make links between aspects of the taught information in science, for example. A group of students may consider changing weather patterns and their physical properties. A more sophisticated network would also encourage the student to make links between the science of weather change and the sociology of climate change, or between the geography of weather patterns and the poetry and literature of drought.

The model presented here is consistent with the findings in *How People Learn.* That report discourages the teaching of disconnected facts because such teaching promotes the organization of knowledge in a random network, the least sophisticated level of knowledge organization. The report also discourages the teaching in separated disciplines. It favors instead the teaching of concepts across disciplines; this approach corresponds to the organization of knowledge around hubs that extend over multiple fields.

What does this mean for actual classroom practice? It is a common practice among informed teachers to discover what students already know before launching into a new topic in the curriculum. Instructional techniques such as KWL (Ogle, 1986) provide a structure within which the teacher can survey what students already know (K), set goals based on what they want to know (W), and survey what they have learned (L). This technique was originally devised as a way to introduce students to a new piece of text by cueing them into the content of the text and giving them a purpose for their reading.

A variety of graphic organizers are available, most of which provide a framework within which students create lists. Lists are inherently linear and may not be the most useful way to activate prior knowledge and encourage the development of complex knowledge networks. Mind maps, on the other hand, are nonlinear and encourage students to relate pieces of information and skills to one another. Such a nonlinguistic and nonlinear graphical organizer can encourage the representation of networks of interrelated knowledge from the earliest point in the curriculum unit. The traditional KWL focuses on the listing of potentially unrelated bits of information. The mind map encourages the recognition and building of complex networks. Both techniques will activate prior knowledge, but mind maps will do so in a way that encourages the development of sophisticated learning.

Prior knowledge assessment is a means to get students to review their knowledge network so they know what they know and then can properly integrate the new information. Mind maps are a means of externally visualizing a format for their knowledge network. The nonlinear nature of mind maps allows the network to be scale free.

The development of a visual learning log is a useful technique for uncovering preconceptions and seeing the interconnectedness of learning. Before you begin a new topic, ask students to help you create a mind map of everything they think they already know. The format is important because it will demonstrate the networked nature of knowledge. This map can be as simple or as complex as the maturity of the students requires. As they develop this map, they will reveal areas where they have very little knowledge or understanding; these should be noted on the map.

At the conclusion of the unit of work, revisit the map, making additions and changes as necessary. In so doing, the class is creating a visual log of their learning, from preconceptions to a more complete understanding. Spend some time with students organizing the learning log by eliminating the misconceptions, identifying the key concepts, and linking the previously known and the newly discovered information with those concepts. Older students could work in small groups to develop a more carefully considered visual learning log to be shared and displayed. This log will also provide a very useful tool for review at exam preparation time.

Students of all ages can practice linking things together. The more these activities cross disciplinary boundaries and those between home and school, the better. One game involves putting three or four unrelated words on the board and looking for ways to link them. The suggestions can be as outlandish or as reasonable as suits the mood and intention of the lesson. It may be just for fun, or it may be an important part of the investigation of a topic. This technique can provide a powerful jump start for creative thinking; we will discuss this further in a later chapter. Just for fun, and to stretch the students' thinking, you might ask them how they could link *snow, algebra,* and *sleeping.* Or perhaps you might ask the students to find links between concepts in a curriculum area; for example, *irrigation, famine,* and *oil.* In both cases, the intellectual task is to find ways of placing each word into a connected network of ideas.

We can help our students recognize the ways in which the worlds inside and outside the school are networked together. Make a list with your beginning readers of all the places they might see written language. The goal here is to help them see how interrelated reading is with the practicalities of daily life as well as the classroom. Older students can look for parallels in their own lives when studying characters in literature or the motivations of historical figures.

We should also seek ways to link curriculum areas and disciplines. How would the work we have been doing in mathematics help us to understand what we are learning in geography? What vocabulary do we have in common?

Understanding that learning is about the building of ever more complex networks and that the learning of one skill can help with the learning of another is an important metacognitive step. Looking for examples of this and then making a visual map of the learning is a useful task. You might ask students how learning to play the piano when they were small helped them do their homework now in Grade 10. This could also draw the Habits of Mind into the notion of an inter-related network as they discuss how the learning of self-discipline and being precise during piano lessons has enabled them to develop good homework habits.

With older students, you might consider giving them a list of words, perhaps drawn from the index of the textbook they are about to begin reading, with a few random words included. The students then work in pairs or small groups to sort the words according to their similarities. Explaining to the rest of the class their reasons for connecting some words together rather than others is an opportunity for them to create a network among previously unorganized items, as well as an opportunity for them access their prior knowledge and to reveal any preconceptions or misconceptions.

Departmentalism and Curriculum Specialization

The pressures of No Child Left Behind legislation in the United States and similar assessment measures in other countries have led to an increasing focus in elementary schools on student achievement as measured by standardized tests in the basic curriculum areas of reading, mathematics, and science. Many states also include testing in history, geography, and civics. In an effort to ensure that the teachers are held responsible for student achievement and are as skilled as possible, there has been an increasing tendency to departmentalize teaching. In some schools, this means that the student will have a different teacher for each subject area; in others, subjects are grouped—science and math in one group, the social studies and English in another. In almost all schools, art, music, and physical education are taught by specialist teachers with specific credentials in these curriculum areas. The unintended consequence of these practices is the fragmenting of the complex network of knowledge organization that would have been possible with true integration of learning. By limiting the formation of links between areas of the curriculum, we are also limiting opportunities to develop the scale-free complex networks that characterize the sophisticated learner. Fragmenting of knowledge is at the random end of the small-world network.

The student who is explicitly encouraged by his teacher to create links between his learning about light and color in science, the collection and manipulation of data in mathematics, the effects of climate and light on the settlement and economic development of a nation, or the use of color in the visual arts and the concept of color in music, will develop a more sophisticated framework for his knowledge through the growth of a scale-free network. The organization of curriculum content around "big questions" that act as hubs results in a knowledge network with no internal limitations on its complexity, and our students move closer toward being sophisticated learners.

Multiple Intelligences

A good football player needs to exercise a number of kinds of intelligence. The use of his interpersonal intelligence enables him to work as a fully functional, responsive team player. Spatial intelligence enables him to predict ball trajectory, player movements, and his own responses. His bodily-kinesthetic intelligence is what makes it possible for him to control and direct his movements effectively during the heat of the game. He needs to make use of his linguistic intelligence to understand the guidance and directives of his coach and communicate strategy with his teammates. His understanding of himself, his motivations, and his reactions to events are mediated by his intrapersonal intelligence.

Effective learning is a kind of team game between the teacher, the student, and the material being learned. A good teacher understands that if a range of intelligences is brought to bear, then learning will be more effective and longer lasting. Robert Marzano has explained the value of nonlinguistic representations as aids to understanding. Students interact with material linguistically, but they also bring their nonlinguistic intelligence to the task, and thereby deepen their understanding (Marzano et al., 2001).

Fifth and sixth graders were helped to understand the difference between the rotation of the earth on its axis and the rotation of the planets around the sun by actually having them out of their seats and demonstrating the differences with their bodies. Older students can enhance their understanding of the poetry of war by comparing, for example, Tchaikovsky's 1812 Overture and its jubilant interpretation of victory with the dark, reflective music of Gorecki's Third Symphony. Allowing students to express their responses to specific poems by means of visual media—painting, drawing, collage, sculpture, and construction—can reveal unexpected richness and sensitivity to the written words. Links need to be made between the ways in which we learn and exercise our various intelligences in order to maximize the complexity of knowledge networks.

Habits of Mind

Many schools have come to understand that effective lifelong learning takes place within the context of certain kinds of intelligent behaviors such as the 16 Habits of Mind of successful people. Teachers who incorporate these habits into their classrooms understand that they do not stand alone as discreet ways of doing things. Instead, they interact and link up with one another, forming complex webs of behavior. One of the habits is about taking responsible risks, another involves taking in data with all the senses, and another involves the ability to think interdependently. The successful individual will make links between these three before deciding to take a particular course of action. Reading, talking with others, and observing the environment all provide data upon which to base the decision to take a responsible risk (Costa & Kallick, 2000).

Bloom's Taxonomy

Benjamin Bloom developed a taxonomy of thinking that has been interpreted as a movement from lower-order to higher-order thinking and a kind of developmental continuum. This linear view of thinking is not helpful in ensuring the creation of rich, complex, scale-free knowledge networks. Knowledge and comprehension are regarded as the foundational cognitive tasks, and analysis, synthesis, and evaluation are considered higher-order cognitive skills. But how can I comprehend anything if I am not able to analyze and evaluate my experiences and decide what is relevant and what is irrelevant? How does a two-year-old speak if he hasn't already listened to all the many and varied sounds he hears, discriminated among them and decided which are significant and which are not, analyzed these sounds, and synthesized them into words—often words that he has never heard before! As the child grows in his language experience, he is able to compare his words with the adult words around him, and adapt and change them until they match more closely—eventually abandoning his baby-talk vocabulary. Every time a two-year-old speaks, he is likely to create a new sentence that he has never heard before. He synthesizes the words he has heard and learned and recombines them in novel ways that serve his purposes. The growth of language is a wonderful example of the interrelatedness of cognitive tasks and the creation of the increasingly complex network we call language.

Skilled teachers will recognize the importance of making links between cognitive tasks rather than seeing them as some kind of developmental sequence that children need to be trained to use.

Curriculum Planning

Curriculum that is carefully planned around the concept of Big Questions makes this kind of linked learning possible. The creation of these plans needs to be done with an open mind. Traditional pro forma planning simply doesn't work. Teachers in schools using this approach frequently choose to create their weekly or monthly lesson planners on large sheets of paper that can be posted on the classroom wall. The planner may incorporate a mind mapping format with the Big Question at its center and a variety of learning tasks as outliers (Wiggins & McTighe, 1998). As teachers create these planners, they are alert to ways they can link different disciplines to deepen student understanding. A tracking chart provides students with different ways of exploring topics and records their choices as well as identifying the kinds of intelligence, Habits of Mind, and cognitive tasks that each learning task has potential to activate.

Each curriculum planner also needs to provide a time at the end of that particular topic for students to reflect on their learning—to metacogitate, to think about their thinking and learning so that they can evaluate it and adjust their learning as necessary. A student may find, on reflection, that his understanding of a topic lacks depth because he didn't keep going when the task became difficult. He may realize that he needs to work on the Habit of Mind of persisting in order to improve the quality of his learning. Another student may discover by looking at the tracking chart that he tends to avoid using his interpersonal intelligence and so misses out on the opportunity to think interdependently (note the link here between one of the multiple intelligences and a Habit of Mind). This can then become a focus for his next learning task.

> In the Resources section, you will find a Metacognitive Planning Template that you can infuse into your existing planning documents.

The work of Canadian educator Lane Clark (http://www.laneclark -ideasys.com/index_new.htm) provides teachers with strategies for the design of curriculum that is focused on the creation of linkages rather than the simplistic notion of learning as a linear, step-by-step process. Additionally, she demonstrates how technology can be seamlessly infused into learning in the classroom. Learning how to design a more holistic curriculum is not a simple task, but it is essential if we are going to assist students in developing the complex networks that characterize the sophisticated learner.

Skilled teachers understand that learning is not purely linear. Students do not learn how to read fluently, understand history, or to play music or a sport simply by moving one step at a time. Learning is not like building a wall, one brick or row at a time. Learning is organic, and it is most effective when teachers explicitly seek links and make them apparent to their students.

Summary

Observations of babies and very young children show a steady increase in the complexity of their thinking and the growing assimilation of new learning into what has already been achieved. We have surveyed a model of how knowledge is organized in the brain that is speculative but based on the nascent science of networks and the results of recent research into brain function. We know that the organization of knowledge and the need for successful integration of new information with old is one of the three findings about successful learning described in the *How People Learn* report. In our classrooms, we should be looking for strategies that encourage the building of ever more complex networks of knowledge rather than the recall of isolated facts and concepts. We need to reassess the ways we structure our schools and separate learning disciplines in departmental organization, curriculum design, and the minds of our students.

THINKING DEEPER: DISCUSSION QUESTIONS

1. What do you need to know in order to be able to read this book with understanding? How is this knowledge organized in your own mind? Can you find a way to visually represent that organization?

2. When you look at the curriculum in your school and in your classroom, what opportunities do you see to link learning in the school with learning outside the school and learning in one discipline with learning in another? How much time do you spend coordinating learning with other teachers?

3. How much do you know about what your students learned last year and what they will learn next year? What bearing does this information have on what you will teach them this year?

4. Consider one concept you are teaching your students this year. What links can you make with skills, ideas, and experiences that are different from that concept and that may have been learned outside of school, in another class, or another year?

9

The Metacognitive Classroom

Let our teaching be full of ideas. Hitherto it has been stuffed only with facts.

—Anatole France

"In our classroom, we know when it is appropriate to stop and think before we act." Is this something that you could say about your current experience of teaching? If both teachers and students are committed to this view of their daily learning, it does not mean that we have a group of navel gazers who feel compelled to analyze and cogitate about every decision. It does mean, however, that they know when it is appropriate to do that. Teachers typically use flash cards to train their students to give automatic responses to factually based questions, such as the names of the continents or multiplication facts. We must ensure that before the flash cards and the automatic response the students have thought about the definition of a continent and what the process of multiplication involves. We must make certain that time is given to thinking in the service of understanding. Once understanding is firmly in place, though, it may be appropriate to commit some information and processes to rote memory.

A classroom becomes thought filled when everyone in it is explicitly aware that *what goes on in one's head is just as important as what is put down on paper.* Of course, the manner in which a five-year-old is aware of the importance of his thinking processes will be very different from that of a college student or an employee learning a new concept or skill. In mathematics, the process is as important as the product. The teacher doesn't simply ask students to get to the answer and give credit when the answer is correct. In a thought-filled classroom, the thinking that led to the answer is the focus of instruction. A teacher in such a classroom is to be heard asking *why* and *how* far more often than *what.* If an answer is incorrect, the student will be asked to consider where the process failed.

In a thought-filled classroom, the purpose of questioning is not only to elicit an answer from a student, but to get the student thinking. In this chapter, we explore the nature of questioning, with the aim of developing the facility of asking questions that promote thinking. Recall Orville Wright's statement (quoted in Chapter 5) about the environment in which he and his brother were raised:

> We were lucky enough to grow up in an environment where there was always much encouragement to children to pursue intellectual interests; to investigate whatever aroused curiosity. In a different environment, our curiosity might have been nipped long before it could have borne fruit.

Questioning

Questioning is a central part of any classroom learning experience. The way you formulate and ask questions can motivate your students to *think before they respond.* Good questioning is a part of good teaching and good learning because it encourages metacognition. Effective teachers understand that it is important to examine *the process* of powerful questioning as well as *the ingredients* of good questions. They compose the major questions they ask with care.

Research into the practices of teachers is revealing. In their book *Quality Questioning: Research-Based Practice to Engage Every Learner,* Walsh and Sattes (2005) describe their recent research, in which they discovered the following:

- Teachers ask a lot of questions—often as many as 50 in 30 minutes
- Students ask very few questions—often as few as 2 in 30 minutes

- Most teacher questions focus on facts and recall; very few require analytical thought
- Not all students are held accountable to respond to questions, and those that do respond are typically the high achievers
- Teachers typically provide less than 1 second for thought after asking a question before calling on a student, and then move on to another student even more quickly
- Teachers tend not to probe incorrect answers

They furthermore found that the teachers they observed waited for more than 3 seconds after asking a question only 12% of the time. Once a student had responded to a question, they found that in 90% of cases teachers waited no time at all before moving on, and frequently were so eager to move forward that they actually interrupted students' responses.

Teaching is more than just telling facts, and learning is more than just remembering; that is why this research is so worrying. We know that the opportunity for students to reflect on and question their new learning in the light of their past experiences is essential to real learning. Learners need to uncover their preconceptions if they are to integrate their new learning with their past experiences. This can best be achieved when teachers ask questions that move beyond the recall of facts and remembered information. Learners need time to formulate their thoughts and find the right language to express them. Language and thought are inextricably intertwined—how do I know what I think until I say it? When we ask questions, we need to provide time for students to formulate their thoughts into explicit language. We also need to give them time to assimilate the language and concepts that we have presented through the content of our questions, to integrate the questions into their own prior understandings. Teachers and students need to learn how to explore and listen to the thoughts of others.

Good questioning is not just a teaching skill; it is also a learning skill. Being able to formulate our own questions is essential to good learning—only the learner knows where there are gaps and spaces in her or his knowledge, and only the learner knows what intrigues. It is important that we teach our students how to ask questions that stimulate and advance their own learning. We must provide them with the time, the structures, and the tools. When designing college exams, we would ask students to design questions that would give them the opportunity to demonstrate what they understood about the topics we had covered, and we would use these questions as a part of their assessment. Over time and with practice, students learned that it was to their advantage to design questions that really challenged and probed their thinking because those were the questions that would be most highly evaluated and gain them the highest grades. When such question designing was included as a teaching strategy, students would be able to uncover the things they did not understand. For each student, this was something different, and their own questions were more effective at uncovering individual problems than teacher-designed questions that were directed to the entire class.

> The Metacognition Monitor in the Resource section provides a structure for older students to question themselves about the effectiveness of their own thinking. This could be simplified for younger students.

How Do We Design Good Questions?

Good questions don't happen by chance. They need to be thought about, planned for, and incorporated into each teaching and learning experience. First, the teacher needs to be clear about the content to be covered. Spend some time clarifying in your own mind the knowledge, concepts, and skills you expect your students to be able to demonstrate at the end of this process. Only by deciding where you expect to be at the end can you be sure to chart a clear and efficient path to that goal. Try not to get too caught up in the details. If something is worth devoting extended time to learning, it needs to be something of significance. Second, be specific about the kinds of thinking skills—cognitive processes—you want to elicit, and ensure that the wording of your questions will direct learners to make use of those types of thinking. If you want students to develop their capacity to make predictions, ask questions that require them to predict. Whenever possible, use the terminology of thinking: "What do you predict will happen if we mix these two substances together?" If you want students to learn about making comparisons, ask, "How would we begin to compare the outcomes of mixing A and B with A and C?"

Third, it is important to encourage learners to increase the complexity and depth of their thinking. The teacher needs to track the levels of thinking required to answer questions and ensure that learners are moving from straightforward recall to the more complex levels of analysis, evaluation, and application. Having identified the factors involved in climate change, for example, thinking moves to a deeper level when learners are asked to predict what might happen if sea levels rose by 2 inches, to analyze the issues involved in moving away from a carbon-based economy, to evaluate arguments about the causes of climate change, or to design a means of overcoming the devastation of drought. At these more profound levels of thinking, learners are not only becoming more adept at thinking, but are also being given the opportunity to engage with their learning and to grapple with the issues and problems about which they are learning.

Finally, good questions will address the behaviors or habits of mind that will be most advantageous in seeking answers. To ask learners to explore the ways in which a problem could be solved encourages them to be flexible thinkers. Asking students "As you read, what do you do when your mind wanders but you want to remain on task?" helps them to develop the ability to manage their impulsivity and at the same time encourages them to think about their thinking—metacognition. Asking "How do you know you are correct?" encourages the student to strive for accuracy. Planning questions that direct attention to these habits of mind infuses the teaching of those behaviors that facilitate skillful thinking into the teaching of content.

Powerful questions induce students to think about cognitive skills and activate appropriate habits of mind. They provide learners with opportunities to practice thinking out loud as they work out their own understandings of new concepts—an important metacognitive skill. Questions offer opportunities for learners to speculate, to explore ideas, to imagine alternatives, and to think flexibly. Well-constructed questions can lead learners to put half-realized thoughts into words and to reflect on what they know and reveal what they don't know. The teacher can direct learners to make links between different areas of learning and integrate new learning with things they have learned in the past.

Creating an environment conducive to productive questioning involves learning how to be a good listener. Research shows us that teachers are too ready to move quickly on to the next student and the next question. Thoughtful responses take time and provide the teacher with opportunities to provoke even deeper reflection.

We have learned much about the attributes of good questioning from working with Arthur Costa and from reading the books written by Costa and Kallick. They demonstrate the richness of thought that can be encouraged by judicious wording and by an approach from the teacher that encourages thought. There are four elements of good questioning; they also require good listening by the teacher. Incorporating these elements into questioning is as valuable to parents and to supervisors as it is to teachers (Costa, 2001). In time, students too will learn how to ask productive questions.

First, we must learn to *slow down.* Mary Budd Rowe tells us in her article "Wait Time: Slowing Down May Be a Way of Speeding Up" (1986) that when we pause and increase the wait time we also increase both the number and the length of responses. Increased wait time encourages the participants to listen to each other and to ask further questions that deepen understanding; in addition, it improves the quality and depth of discussions.

The second element of effective questioning is *paraphrasing.* This does not mean simply repeating what the other person has said back to them. Instead, it involves rephrasing what the listener has heard into his or her own words and then seeking confirmation that there is real understanding. The questioner might begin by saying something like this: "I find it very interesting that you think that . . ." or "When you say that . . . are you thinking of something very different from what Aaron said?" Paraphrasing in this way shows the speaker that you are interested in and value what they have to say and that you are striving to understand them. It also provides an opportunity to identify and correct any misunderstandings or fuzzy thinking. It encourages metacognition.

The third aspect of effective questioning is *probing.* When you ask a question, receive a response, and then ask a follow-up question that develops the answer you have been given, you are doing a number of things. You are demonstrating respect for the ideas of the other person by showing that what they said was interesting and valuable enough that you want to know more. By strengthening the relationship in this way, you help create an environment in which the learner feels safe enough to take the risks that are essential for significant learning to take place. Probing questions provide clarification to the listener and to the person who responded to the question. Often, our first responses are not our best, and a well-designed question that grows out of that first response can push us to think more deeply. Probing questions encourage us to communicate with greater clarity and precision. When a student is asked what he knows about Mount Everest and he responds with "Well, it's really big and stuff," a follow-up question that explores the student's understanding of the size of Everest can lead to more precise language use and start him along a path to learning more about the mountain by refining his understandings.

The fourth element requires the teacher to *refrain from making judgments.* When a teacher asks a class a question and someone offers an answer that clearly pleases or gains the approval of the teacher, thinking closes down. If the teacher manages to express an accepting acknowl-edgment rather than making any judgments about the correctness of a response, the responder and the listeners in the class have no good reason to stop thinking, because they have not been given any sense yet that they are at the end of this particular exploratory road. Consider these two different scenarios:

Teacher 1:   Who knows why feelings about drought and the desire for rain are so prominent in Australian literature?

Student: Because it's a really arid country.

Teacher 1:   That's right, John. Thanks. Anyone else?

. . . Silence

Teacher 2:   Who knows why feelings about drought and the desire for rain are so prominent in Australian literature?

Student A: Because it's a really arid country

Teacher 2:   Anyone else?

Wait time

Student B: Maybe it's because agriculture is an important part of life.

Student C: Yeah. Crops don't grow without rain.

Wait time

Student D: So why did they try and grow crops if it really doesn't rain?

Student E: Do they really rely on crops? I thought they imported all their grain and vegetables and only produced sheep.

Teacher 2:   How would we go about answering that question?

Student E: We could check out major imports to Australia in our text book.

Teacher 1 has closed down conversation and thought by accepting the first answer as correct. Teacher 2, on the other hand, has made no comment about correctness or incorrectness; instead, the students are free to make tentative hypotheses and then are encouraged to find ways of evaluating their ideas. The students' knowledge networks are encouraged to grow as new links are added to the original question.

The most effective teachers know that questioning is not simply about discovering what information their students have remembered. They understand the potential of well-formed questions to promote thinking.

There are many nonverbal elements to effective questioning. When we are confronted with a verbal message that says one thing but nonverbal cues that seem to suggest something else, we are much more inclined to accept the meaning behind the nonverbal cues. Telling a child that you are sorry a favorite toy has been broken in rough play means one thing to the child when you tower over him, use a loud "no-nonsense" voice, and have your arms firmly crossed in front of you. It means something quite different to him when you get down to his level, make eye contact, reach out and touch his shoulder; and use a softer, more intimate intonation. They are the same words but carry two very different messages.

Types of Questions

Too often, when we ask questions we play a game called "I know the answer. Do you?" Implied in the form of the question is the assumption that there is only one correct answer and that once it has been elicited we can all move on. In some circumstances that might be a fine strategy, but it doesn't work when our goal is to encourage thinking.

Multiple Possibilities

Questions need to be constructed so that they allow the possibility of multiple answers. By making them both plural and somewhat tentative, we invite thoughtful exploration. "What is the answer to this problem?" assumes only one correct answer and shuts down thinking to a single track. "What might be some possible answers to this problem?" leaves the doors to thought open.

Expectations

Our presuppositions are very powerful because they communicate much about our expectations. Learners live both *up to* and *down to* the expectations of those around them. Questions can both empower and disempower; learning is best achieved when the learner believes he can succeed. Asking "Do you have a goal for this class?" allows the possibility that the student might simply dismiss it by saying "No." A door is closed. The question could be rephrased so that it reflects some more empowering presuppositions; for example, "As you thought about this class, what were some of the goals you came up with?" This assumes that we believe the student has been thinking about the class already, and that there could be not one but many acceptable goals. The question assumes the best of the student and invites him to respond without a sense of being judged right or wrong.

Thinking Skills

Sometimes we need to design questions that will encourage students to engage specific thinking skills. We may want them to have more experience

- gathering data: *Where could we go to find some more information?*
- making comparisons: *What other machines might operate the same way as this one?*
- evaluating ideas: *What might be some fair solutions to this problem?*
- speculating about complex problems: *What do you think might happen if we closed down this major road through the town?*

Questions may focus on the world outside the student, on social issues, or on curriculum content. At other times, we may want to design questions that lead the learner to focus on what is going on inside, to explore his own thinking strategies or his own emotions. By asking the student to think of other ways to solve the problem, we encourage flexible thinking. Asking a student to explain how he knows his solution is correct requires him to strive for accuracy. The question "If you were John, how would you react to what you said about him?" encourages listening with empathy and understanding, and asking "When you find yourself tempted to respond emotionally to a situation, what alternatives do you consider?" helps a person to manage impulsivity and to think more flexibly.

Whatever it may be, having a clear purpose for our questions helps us to make productive decisions about question design and the kinds of interactions we have with people when we are engaged in these sorts of discussions. Teachers who write out their key questions before the lesson are more likely to design questions that have a clearly articulated purpose in their lesson planning.

But skillful questioning is not just something for teachers. It is for all of us. Thoughtful questions lead to deeper metacognition. In order to ask a good question about a subject, the material itself needs to be well understood. Questioning is valuable, too, because it reveals what we do not know; the acknowledgment of not knowing something must be seen as an important part of learning.

There are many classroom situations that can encourage students to ask questions. Role playing provides opportunities to become a reporter or an interviewer. Students can design questions before they have a classroom visitor and can be allowed to design their own class quizzes when a topic has been completed. In the home, it is important to make time for questions. Parents can be driven to distraction by the constant questions of a very young child, but keep in mind that this small person is immersed in a world full of brand-new sensations and events. These questions are all part of the child's attempt to make sense of it all. What may seem obvious to you is only obvious because you have already worked it all out. Young children are newcomers to the planet. Give them time. Use their questioning as an opportunity to deepen their thinking by probing and by asking carefully designed, nonthreatening follow-up questions.

Four-year-old Child:	Why did the duck go under the water?
Parent:	What do you think might be under the water?
Child:	Stuff.
Parent:	What kind of stuff?
Child:	Mud.
Parent:	Do you think some things might live in that mud?
Child:	I don't know. Maybe bugs and fish.
Parent:	Well, there are a lot of creatures that live in the mud; beetles, grubs, all sorts of stuff.
Child:	Does the duck like to eat them?
Parent:	We could find out a lot more about ducks at the library.

In this interaction, the parent has encouraged the child to think more deeply and provided a means to discover more information. It would have been easy to simply say "It's looking for food," and often that might be the most appropriate kind of response. But if you want to help your child become a skillful thinker, give plenty of opportunities to practice thinking.

Our adolescent children are struggling to make moral sense of the world. They can sense their independence in the near future when they will no longer have the protection of their parents. That can be both exhilarating and frightening. In order for them to develop their own moral compasses, they need to imagine sailing in many directions. By providing information while refraining from judgment, by listening with empathy and questioning thoughtfully, we can keep the dialogue open and help our children understand themselves and the world better as they chart their own courses.

Summary

Classrooms are places of inquiry, and effective questioning is at the heart of successful teaching and deep learning because it encourages metacognition. A skilled teacher knows how to ask questions that motivate students to interrogate their own thinking, to question their answers, and understand how they formulated those answers. Learners also need to know how to ask probing questions that enrich their own thinking and lead them further along the path to becoming independent, flexible thinkers and learners able to operate productively and confidently in a complex world.

THINKING DEEPER: DISCUSSION QUESTIONS

1. The way we form our questions can activate specific types of thinking and specific habits of mind. How might you ask a question if you want your students to compare several things and evaluate them?

2. Imagine that you have set students a cooperative task to complete. Each student is required to write a report at the conclusion that incorporates the contributions of everyone. You suspect that one student has not done this and has only used his own ideas. How might you ask questions that would open up the students' thinking and encourage him to examine his own habits of mind as well as the effectiveness of his thinking strategies?

3. What kinds of questions do your students ask?

4. Of whom do they typically ask them?

5. What might you do to encourage your students to ask more questions themselves?

10

Two Powerful Classroom Tools

The object of teaching a child is to enable him to get along without his teacher.

—Elbert Hubbard

Note Takers or Note Makers?

As we have emphasized, brain research tells us that one of the most important parts of learning is the organization of new knowledge and its integration into what the brain already knows. It is important to understand facts and ideas within a conceptual framework. We have all heard of the notion of multiple intelligences. We know that students have different styles of thinking and of learning; for example, some students are better visual learners than others and need to represent their knowledge in images, whereas others need to get it written out before they can really understand something.

Traditionally, note taking in the classroom or the lecture hall has been a process of recording information, usually the opinions or observations of our teachers or others. One graduate student explained this to us:

> As a school student and later at university I filled books with the carefully written notes that would form the foundation of my studying for the inevitable exams at the end of the semester or academic year. I devised a very efficient manner of studying where I would progressively summarize my notes, topic by topic, page by page, and paragraph by paragraph until I was left with just a set of letters that would become a mnemonic for a vast underlying pool of knowledge. When I entered the exam room, I would write down the mnemonic sentence as soon as we were permitted to lift our pens. I would then expand each letter and each word until I had recreated my year's work. The initial letters of each word in the mnemonic sentence would stand for a word that in turn led to other sentences, paragraphs and pages of information lurking below the surface of my mind. This system worked well for me. I became a skilled "rememberer," and passed my exams with flying colors, but I didn't learn to think this way.

In a thought-filled classroom, note making can serve as a platform for thinking. Of course, notes will still be a valuable resource when preparing for exams, but the act of note making itself will be a part of the processes of learning—the exploring, inventing, testing, and challenging that characterize real learning. Note making becomes a *thinking* activity.

The method of note making we are describing here can be adapted to serve students from primary schooling to advanced university study. The principles are the same; only the level of complexity needs to be adjusted. The thinking notebook is set up in a very structured manner. The ways in which the structure is used are limited only by the ingenuity of the teacher and the creative thinking of the students.

What Kind of Notebook?

Students will need a sturdy notebook with binding that can accommodate the additional thickness that results from pasting notes to pages. Loose-leaf folders are not advisable because it becomes too easy to remove a page if a student is tempted to create a visually attractive notebook rather than a truly useful tool. Because there will be a great deal of thinking involved, and not all thinking will be well organized, pages can become messy and disorganized too. Past experiences may encourage some students to feel that an untidy page is somehow a failure, and they may want to get rid of the evidence. A thought-filled classroom values thinking, and its members understand that we learn from messy thinking as well as from moments of razor-sharp insight. Our students need to be helped to understand that the *process* is valuable; the notebook is a valuable record of the process.

Setting It Up

Number every page, and leave the first few pages to create a table of contents. As the notebook grows, students will be able to use the table of contents to help review past learning as they move ahead into new territory. Numbering the pages ahead of time also discourages the student from pulling pages out and hence losing the record of their thinking.

The Right-Hand Side: The Recording Page

The teacher provides the content of the lesson—the key information, vocabulary, and concepts that are to be covered—as a concise page of notes that the student will paste onto the right-hand page of a double page of the notebook. Older students may generate this key information themselves. These notes can include vocabulary lists, explanations, definitions, conceptual information, demonstrations of procedures, textbook notes, film or video notes, guest speaker notes, and such. This information involves more of the left hemisphere of the brain: it is analytical, sequential, logical, and linguistic.

Annotation of Notes

Students will interact with the notes their teacher has provided (or those they have made themselves) by using lots of color to underline, highlight, and circle sections of the text. They need to have a clear scheme; for example, red highlighter for unknown words, blue highlighter for all key words, underlining for topic sentences, circling of intriguing phrases or sentences—the ones that pique the student's interest. Students should have developed and recorded a color key in their notebooks; for older students, it is a good idea to let them devise their own.

Here is a sixth-grade example of an annotated science page:

Figure 10.1	An example of an annotated text where main ideas are underlined and numbered, key words colored, and notes for further consideration have been made

① Matter can undergo a physical change from one state to another: solid, liquid or gas. When a material changes from a solid to a liquid, the process is called melting, and occurs at a temperature called the melting point, which is specific to the given substance. The liquid can change back to a solid by freezing and this temperature is called the freezing point. When a liquid boils, it vaporizes and becomes a gas.

Is a vapor the same as a gas?

what's the difference? Review

② The particles (atoms or molecules) of a material in each of these three states, have different properties. In a solid they are held together very tightly and have little room to move; in a liquid, the particles have more energy that in a solid state and are able to move around more. In a gas, particles are not held together at all and are able to move around completely. They have much more energy and move more quickly than those in the other two states.

define this

The Left-Hand Page: The Creative Processing and Thinking Page

This is where the organization and integration of learning takes place. This is the thinking side, the place where the students are required to process and represent their developing knowledge in *new* ways. Using all their classroom experiences—the notes on the right-hand page, classroom discussions, experiments, field trips, videos, reference reading, past learning, learning in other subject areas—the student reframes his new learning in diagrams, tables, mind maps, pictures, and other nonlinguistic forms. He rephrases concepts into his own language, sorts and arranges information using tables and Venn diagrams, uses arrows to create cycles or cause-and-effect diagrams, writes poems, and asks questions. Frequently, he is drawing on the right-hand side of his brain—the visual, creative side.

While it is essential that every student's notebook has the same information on the right-hand page, the left-hand pages will look different because each student is given the opportunity to interpret the information in a manner most suited to his learning style and drawing on his own creativity. At the end of a lesson, the students may write a reflection on what has been learned, draw a picture that illustrates the central points of the lesson, or ask questions that have either arisen or failed to be answered during the lesson. Students use this page to reflect on, explain, and justify their learning. It becomes a portfolio of learning experiences. Here is the same sixth-grade student's left-hand page:

Figure 10.2	The student has used nonlinguistic pictures to represent the main ideas in the text.

Here is an example by an older student using the thinking notebook in a literature class:

> **Figure 10.3** On this double page, we see the textual information on the right-hand side and the student's restatement of the main ideas in diagrams and drawings on the left-hand page.

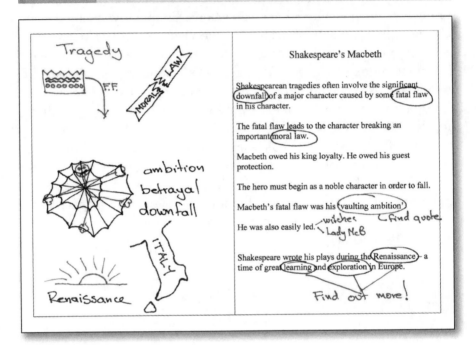

The Teacher's Role

In addition to providing the notes for the right hand-page, the teacher needs to teach the students how to use their notebooks. Initially, students may need to be given a great deal of direction about the sorts of activities they can engage in on the left-hand page. They may need to be taught how to construct Venn diagrams, tables appropriate for representing particular types of information, mind maps, or poems. It can be helpful if the teacher suggests and lists particular activities for each lesson, gradually increasing the number of options as students become more familiar and comfortable with the method of note making and moving to a point where students make their own choices about how to reframe, organize, and structure their knowledge.

It is very important that lessons be planned to include time for constructing the notebook. Left-page work needs to become an essential, valued, and anticipated part of most lessons. Reasons also need to be given for students to look back through their notebooks, either to retrieve information or to compare their current thinking and understanding with that of weeks or months earlier.

The teacher should regularly collect and review the notebooks. Only by doing so is it possible to know which students are struggling with the integration of new knowledge or misunderstanding key concepts. We can assure you that when the thinking notebooks are being used well you will be fascinated by their content!

This technique can also be used in less formal situations in which students are exploring ideas or learning new material; it is not always necessary to actually compile a notebook. The simplest, single-page note making can be just as interactive. Here is a photograph of a Girl Scout's notes taken during a NASA Saturday science session we gave on the concept of speed:

Figure 10.4   On the right-hand side we see the statement that velocity is a measure of speed and the direction of motion. On the left-hand side are two images: the points of the compass representing direction and a speedometer representing velocity in the student's mind. The verbal information has been recast in a nonlinguistic manner.

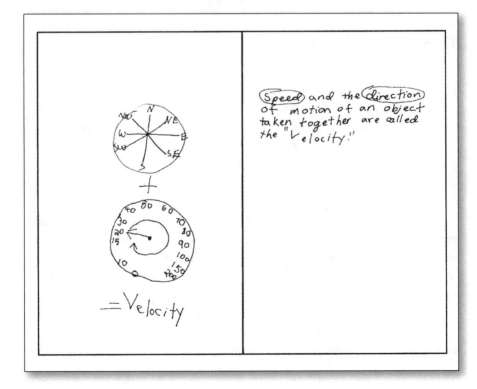

Interactive Learning

As we have described, the two hemispheres of the brain have somewhat different functions. The left side of the brain is the logical hemisphere: it is analytical, rational, and is particularly involved in language. The right side of the brain is the creative and intuitive hemisphere, gathering information from images, interpreting patterns and body language, emotional content, and tone of voice. We often hear people describe themselves as either left-brained or right-brained, but in reality we all use both sides of our brains, and we learn best when both sides work together to analyze and synthesize experiences and information. The thinking notebook reflects the organization of the brain in that the right-hand side is logical, linguistic, and analytical, and the left-hand side provides an opportunity to work on that information in more personal, creative, and interpretative ways.

The thinking notebook is sometimes described as an *interactive* notebook because it provides a medium for students to interact with their learning and make it their own at a deeper, more thoughtful, and more integrated level. Students are no longer simply note takers; they become note *makers* and thinking learners who use their notes as a way of learning, rather than simply a record of what should be learned for a future test or examination.

Thoughtful Assessment

When a teacher who values thinking grades mathematics papers, she looks closely at the calculations and gives credit for correct work as well the correct answer. Thinking is devalued when a teacher marks as wrong an expanded process that demonstrates understanding but contains a single miscalculation. The answer may be wrong, but the thinking may be right. If thinking is valued then the teacher must find a way of indicating this to her students in the way she grades mathematics papers. Of course, accuracy is important too.

The teaching of spelling is an important part of the literacy program in the early years of schooling. Weekly spelling tests are often given, parents are always eager to know how well their children performed in spelling, and a great deal of effort is put into helping parents understand that children go through a similar process of discovery and invention mastering the written language as they did when learning to talk. The invented spellings of the five- and six-year-old are very much like the mispronounced words of the two-year-old. We know that with continued exposure to correct models and lots of encouragement, our children will gradually come to spell words the traditional way.

We help them along the way with directed teaching of spelling rules and tricks and techniques to help work out how unfamiliar words might be spelled. When a teacher shows children how to spell *elephant*, they might look for any other words that have the rather odd spelling pattern *ph*. What should a teacher do if a child writes *ellephant* on a test? Such a response should give us cause to stop, think, and reassess what we are doing when we grade spelling. The child had paid attention during the lesson; she had remembered the *ph* sound, she had gotten first and last letters correct, and she had the right number of syllables. She had gotten this much right because she was thinking as she wrote the word and remembering what she had already been taught. She also knew that some words have double consonants in them and that a double *l* was common. She knew a lot, and she had thoughtfully applied what she knew to this new word. How could a teacher simply take a red pencil and mark an X next to her attempt? To do so would be to devalue all the thinking she had done.

If a classroom is a place where thinking is valued, we need to develop different grading practices, perhaps by placing a tiny check mark above each correct letter and circling the letters that were incorrect. This child had got eight things correct and only one thing incorrect when she wrote *ellephant*. Her correct thinking would thus be acknowledged, and she would be aware of exactly where she had gone wrong. Classrooms must demonstrate to students that we value their thinking and not simply their ability to produce a correct end product.

Assessment tasks can also be extended thinking and learning tasks if we provide opportunities for students to reflect and then rework their tests. Too often, tests are graded and handed back, and the only thing the students take any notice of is the grade—the number or letter written by the teacher in the top right-hand corner. The purpose of the exercise has become judgment, not learning. This is a wasted opportunity.

Thinking About How to Study

Assessment can also be used as a powerful opportunity for metacognition. By encouraging students to think about how they study, we can provide opportunities for them to understand, monitor, evaluate, and adjust their behaviors in the light of their results on tests.

Often, students make poor choices about how they study because they are unaware of alternatives and their consequences. To investigate students' behaviors and attitudes on study for a particular course, one of the authors (Martin) took two specific actions on tests. First, as each test was handed in, he noted the time spent on the test, and then graphed the grade earned versus time taken. The result from one test, shown in Figure 10.5, was typical of results on other tests. This graph indicates that generally the more time taken on an exam, the better the resulting grade; specifically, an additional 10 minutes spent working the exam typically resulted in a grade increase of about 6 points.

The second action was to place the following extra question on each exam:

During this middle part of the course I have been spending, on average,

- one hour per week
- two hours per week
- three hours per week
- more than three hours per week

studying for this course.

This question was graded as correct for all students who answered it; it was assumed that students were generally truthful. The results are shown in Figure 10.6. The average study time was 2.3 hours per week. It is clear from the graph that grades generally increased with an increase in study time. Basically, spending 2 hours per week in study instead of 1 hour will increase your grade by about 6 points.

The conclusions shown in these two graphs are not surprising. We all know that if you want to increase your grade, you work harder. The graphs make it possible to quantify the improvement that a specific increase in a student's effort will produce. Students were confronted with concrete evidence from their own experience, which showed approximately how much their grade would change if they worked longer. Most students were surprised by these results. They seemed not to be able to assess the consequences of changes in their behavior because they were not used to thinking metacognitively about their studying practices. They did not have the language to think about how their effort could influence their scholastic outcomes.

Note taking and assessment are both significant tasks within any classroom. If the teacher has a clear focus on thinking as the basis of learning, they can both become powerful tools encouraging a meta-cognitive approach to learning.

Figure 10.5	This graph shows the grade earned on an exam versus the time taken to complete the exam. A linear regression line is also shown.

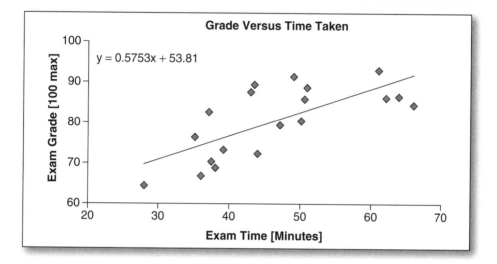

Figure 10.6	This graph shows the exam grade for a test on material covered in a five-week period versus the average number of hours spent in study over that period. The line is drawn to emphasize the two groups of data.

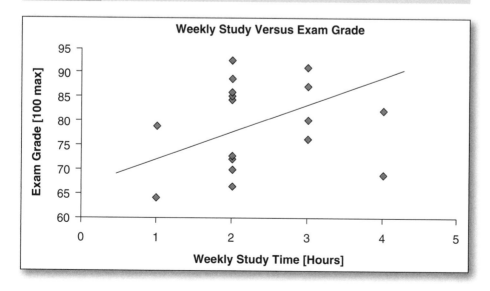

Summary

From their earliest years at school, students are asked by their teachers to make records of their learning in notes of some sort. We have provided you with a guide to the creation of notes that are more than collections of information and practice examples. Note making can become a powerful thinking tool, incorporating proven learning strategies and making good use of what we have learned about how the brain works. It allows for the individual learning styles of different students. As students become proficient, it increasingly encourages them to think metacognitively about their own learning in order to decide how best to interact with the material and ideas with which they are currently working. We have also examined the grading or marking techniques used by teachers and suggested how, with adaptation, these too can do more than judge, but can also demonstrate that thinking is valued by the school and encourage students to think ever more deeply.

11

Creating A Metacognitive Learning Community

School and Home

A school is a highly complex and dynamic community. It changes in subtle ways as it responds to the changing pressures and demands placed on it at different times in the school year. The hallways feel very different just before testing periods than they do during the last week of the school year. Many experienced teachers will swear that the school changes character on windy days! Provided the school is an *actively learning* community, this dynamism can not only be dealt with, it can become the lifeblood that gives the place its vibrancy and vigor.

How do we ensure that a school is an actively learning community and not a rigid organization operating within a set of largely immutable rules and traditional principles and practices? We need to ensure that all the members of this community are engaged. There should be no sense that somehow education is someone else's responsibility. Different groups of participants within the institution will play different roles, and those roles may well change over time, but everyone is a part of the community and a contributor to the process. Parents, ancillary staff, administrators, teachers, and students are all part of the tapestry that is a school. Each provides a different thread of a different color, but they are woven together to form the fabric that is the school.

Creating a Culture

For this sense of community to exist, there must be a sense of shared beliefs and values about what it is that we are trying to achieve. It is this shared foundation that will give the fabric of the school its structure and its strength. This doesn't mean we need to agree politically, religiously, or about what is the best way to get our children to eat vegetables. But it does mean that we agree about the fundamentals of what we are trying to achieve in our school. In this chapter, we will explore some of the ways in which teachers, administrators, and parents are able to contribute to this learning community and create a culture of metacognition.

Members of a community share each other's values and attitudes. They do not think identically, but there is a core of commonality about what they believe is important, what can be tolerated, what are the things to which they aspire. Importantly, these values and expectations are made explicit and shared with both students and their parents. It is inevitable and desirable that there will be variations in the ways that individuals interpret and enact these shared values, but it is essential that the values be shared.

How you deal with individuals who are unable to share the school's values will depend in part on the staffing practices of your school district. This is part of preparing the ground for the successful cultivation of a thinking school. If your values are clearly stated, applicants for positions in the school will be aware from the beginning of the expectations they must meet. Those who are already members of your staff may have to make some difficult decisions if they find that they are unable to embrace the culture. Remember, though, that if you focus on the successes of those who do reflect the culture, and if the positive outcomes of a school that values thinking are evident, the initially reluctant will often find opportunities to be flexible and begin to support their colleagues. School leaders need to be patient, provide support rather than censure, and demonstrate rather than lecture. But in the end they may need to make some firm decisions.

Difficulties can arise when we consider a school where some teachers may have a limited range of teaching strategies that truly engage students. There may be discipline problems, and raised voices can become the order of the day as you walk the hallways. It is hard to create anything lasting with a background of barely contained chaos. There is a clear need to work hard to develop strategies that make students active participants rather than passive listeners. Initially, some teachers may be anxious, believing that if they give these students an inch by allowing them to talk and move about in the classroom, they will take a mile, and classrooms will dissolve into disorder. But slowly, as they implement some of these new strategies into their daily programs, they will discover that because students are no longer bored they are becoming less inclined to be disruptive. As the quality of teaching improves, the number of discipline issues will decline.

There may be some teachers who are not able or willing to make these changes. Their limited repertoire of teaching strategies mean that their students remain disengaged and the teacher's voice may still be heard thundering along the hallways as the battle for classroom control continues. In the end, perhaps a firm and clear conversation is needed between administrator and teacher, insisting that there will be no shouting in the school unless someone is in danger. Unfortunately, it is sometimes necessary to make it explicit that if a teacher has not embraced the culture of a school community, the time has come to consider his future.

It is important, too, that parents understand and contribute to this culture, because they are a part of the community, and that community's values must be in alignment with their values. In districts where parents are able to make choices about the schools to which they will send their children, this is much easier. The culture of the school should be made evident in the physical surroundings, the communications, and the general tone of the school when a visitor comes through the front door. When you walk through the entrance of a metacognitive school, you should be immediately aware that this school values thinking. It will be apparent in the wording of the school vision or mission as it is posted on the notice board. Signs and directions around the school will encourage all members of the community to be thoughtful participants in the school's activities. Posters will challenge people to reassess their assumptions, and there will be invitations to participate in an ongoing discussion about learning and teaching. A suggestion box in the front office is a simple way for parents to participate. Many schools have a motto and a symbol that sets their school apart from all others. Make sure that your school icons and slogans reflect the school's belief that thinking is at the heart of its educational practices.

Every effort should be made to ensure that parents understand the culture of the school before they make any decisions about registering their children. In school districts that practice zoning, this can be much more difficult. Parents may not understand, and in some cases may not initially agree with, the beliefs that underlie the practices of the school. Communication and inclusion are the means to developing a parent community that supports the ideals of the school. As the professional educators who have the responsibility to make the decisions about the school, administrators and teachers must communicate a commonly held set of beliefs and provide ample opportunities to work with parents. We have a responsibility to be articulate and explain why we do things the way we do.

Developing a Culture of Metacognition in the School

The word *culture* comes from the Latin word *cultura*, meaning "to cultivate." As generally used, we take it to refer to the shared attitudes, values, goals, and practices that we have already mentioned. This culture does not come easily, nor is it a given that once established it will flourish. It needs to be *cultivated.* The ground needs to be prepared carefully, the ideas need to be sown, then fertilized and watered regularly. We need to be on the lookout for weeds—the naysayers who can undermine our best efforts, and signs of wilt—the fatigue or complacency that can develop if both the ideas and the members of the community are not nurtured. Culture is a process, not an outcome.

Preparation of the ground for a culture of metacognition begins by working to ensure that all participants share a common sense of purpose. Parents, teachers, and administrators will have come to a broad agreement about a shared set of objectives for their endeavors. Has your school initiated this discussion? Are you sure that your sense of purpose is compatible with that of your principal? Do the parents of the students you teach have the same view as you of the purposes behind the activities in your classroom? Do you just want your students to pass the tests at the end of the year, or would you like to think that your efforts produce some long-term benefits that will still be present and growing five years after the students leave your care and influence? What really matters in your school and in your classroom? Where are these outcomes stated explicitly in your curriculum? How do your lesson plans ensure that these things are taught *with intentionality?* Start the discussion!

Parents and Teachers Working Together

Even the most financially stretched and emotionally stressed parents want the best for their children. They want their children to have better lives that they did. Parents who are already actively involved in their children's education need reassurance that they are on the right track, that they are supplementing and supporting what goes on at school. If one of our primary goals in school is to develop students who can think metacognitively and understand how they learn, how they can monitor their thinking, evaluate its effectiveness, and modify it when necessary, we need to show parents how they can play their part.

We can have strategies in place at school to mitigate some of the negative effects that difficult times at home can have on learning in the classroom. But we can do much more. Johns Hopkins University put in place a National Network of Partnership Schools in 1996. The purpose of this developing and growing network is to encourage and facilitate cooperation between schools, districts, states, and organizations as they work to educate our young people. Research has shown that when parents feel involved and engaged in their children's education, their children do better. Readers can discover more about this program on the Johns Hopkins University web site at http://www.csos.jhu.edu/p2000.

Bringing up children is a complex task and, as has often been bemoaned by both new and experienced parents, the recently acquired laptop and toaster both came with operating manuals, but the baby didn't. So how do we help parents understand how best to raise metacognitive children? What suggestion can we provide that will encourage parents to create an environment in the home where children thrive and apply thought to the tasks and problems of growing up?

If they are fortunate, new parents have more experienced parents close by who can support and guide. There are playgroups, new parent support groups, and community and welfare groups where the new parent can find advice. Bookshops and libraries are stocked with shelves full of books on parenting. A quick glance at Amazon.com's titles on parenting revealed they had 63,399 titles! A parent might be lucky enough to discover a title among all of these that provides insights into how to raise a metacognitive child, but it would take a lot of hard work and no small amount of luck, given the size of field.

What Are Our Priorities?

As more and more is added to the mandated curriculum, it is understandable if teachers lift up their hands in dismay and cry "Whoa! Enough is enough. We don't need any more." That is precisely why we argue that the teaching of skillful thinking, and the teaching of metacognition in particular, is a process and not yet another piece of content. Learning to be metacognitive thinkers is about *how* we do things, *how* we teach, *how* we learn, and *how* we operate in the home. By making it a part of the culture, we infuse it into everything that we do, both at school and at home.

Just as teachers do, parents find that time is a commodity in short supply. Many families today have two working parents. Preschool children and infants may spend time in childcare settings in which they vie for attention in a group larger than the usual family group. At the end of the day, children are collected, taken home, fed, bathed, and put to bed. Mom and Dad may be weary from their day at work; children may be fractious and competing with each for the attention of their parents. It is little wonder, then, that some parents find themselves looking forward to the moment when they can flop into a chair in front of the TV with the kids tucked into bed. Parents with lighter financial burdens may seem to have more time at their disposal and yet find their children's time filled up with tennis and piano lessons, homework requirements, and, as they get older, the many social demands that fill the spare hours of teenagers' lives.

At some point, both educators and parents need to stop and reevaluate. We want the best for our communities and our children. We will only achieve this if we make it a priority to develop the next generation into people who think rather than always firing from the hip, who respond thoughtfully rather than reacting instinctively, who consider and then act rather than acting first and thinking later. "I've made up my mind, don't confuse me with facts" is not amusing any more. It lies at the root of prejudice, violence, and social inequality. It is the mantra of a closed mind. We have the opportunity to make sure our children's minds remain open so that they continue to think, and think skillfully, about the world around them. That is an opportunity too good and too important to miss. We must make it a high priority and give it the time it deserves. This is a dialogue we must begin as a matter of urgency and keep at the heart of everything we do.

Creating Times and Places to Talk and Reflect

Finding time within a school day is often a matter of clever scheduling to ensure that there are regular, significant periods of time available for teachers to meet and share ideas. It is alarmingly easy for these times to become filled with "administrivia." A degree of formality, with an agenda and a delegated person each meeting to provide a short summary of discussions, can help overcome this. Teachers of a common year level need to communicate regularly, but meetings also need to cross both year levels and subject disciplines. The development of community is not facilitated by the presence of introverted, isolated cells. We all need to talk together.

The student body can be helped to develop a sense of community as well by means of regular schoolwide assemblies. It is hard for children to develop a relationship with a disembodied voice on a public address system. Assemblies, to which parents are welcomed and which allow the participation of various groups, develop cohesion. It can provide a time to make explicit and explore the values of the school community.

> In the Resources section of this book you will find a list of suggested activities and organizational hints that will help make whole-school assemblies positive and productive experiences.

Communication with parents needs to emphasize the fact that perhaps the most important things children need from parents are time to talk and for their parents to listen. Thinking takes time. We do not think well when we are under pressure to "get on with it." Young children and adolescents both are faced with a complex and changing society. Understanding and finding their way successfully through that society will inevitably take time. They will be successful if parents guide them and safeguard time together to talk, to think, to ask questions, and to consider possibilities.

The establishment of a garden area with shady trees and some benches around a table can be signposted as the "Thinking Place" and be available to any members of the school community who need a quiet spot to thrash out some contentious or problematic issue. Similarly, a parent meeting room within the school that has coffee-making facilities, books, a computer, and a printer tells parents that they are valued and the school invites their participation. By selecting books and magazines that stimulate thinking about learning, and by the way the room is decorated with posters and thought-provoking sayings, we are creating a physical environment that speaks to a culture of thought, discussion, and cooperation.

Too often, parents' groups feel that their only function is to help raise funds for the school. In some schools, this attitude can be deeply entrenched; if this is the case in your school, consider suspending all fundraising activities for a period of time, so that you can focus on parents as partners in the education of their children. It can also help to arrange some regular, scheduled meetings between administrators, parents, and teachers. Monthly morning coffee meetings at which parents are invited to set the agenda and the principal and available teachers participate as listeners and contributors demonstrate that dialogue is valued, as is the sharing of ideas. Parents can be asked via the newsletter for a set of topics that can then provide a focus for each meeting. Setting an agenda helps provide direction, but parents need to feel ownership in this process as well. If we want to have parents as valued partners, we need to walk a fine line between guiding these meetings and dominating them.

Parents as Partners in Metacognition, in the Resources section of this book, is a set of planning points for conversations between parents and the school.

Finding the Right Time

Not everything needs to be discussed, and sometimes children need to simply accept guidance and do as they are told. A teacher dealing with an out-of-control five-year-old hiding under a desk or a potentially violent adolescent on the playground, or a parent negotiating cars while crossing the street in a busy city, do not have the time for a discussion about the pros and cons of tears as a response to criticism, aggression as a solution to conflict, or holding a parent's hand in traffic. Putting fragile items on top shelves is a wiser tactic than trying to explain to a toddler about the personal nature of objects and the fragility of crystal.

Consider this scene. An enraged two-year-old is ripping her twin sister's paintings off the living-room wall. In a misguided attempt to encourage the child to think about her actions, her father follows behind her and asks questions such as "How do you think Mary is going to feel when she sees what you have done? How would you feel if these were your paintings?" Of course, the little girl simply continues ripping up the paintings. This was not the time for a thoughtful discussion. This was the time for the father to simply take the child, remove her from the situation, and give her time to cool down without causing any more damage. There will be many opportunities in the future for this father to quietly, and perhaps incidentally, direct his daughter to examine her own feelings, to take notice of others, and speculate about how they may be feeling. As she matures, she will gradually develop empathy, an important aspect of thought-filled behavior. We need to consider the timing of our attempts to encourage our young people to think about their actions as well as the maturity of the child.

The Power of Questions

If we are learning together, we will be asking each other questions. Questions are powerful, and while the well-formed question can create a bond between two people and lead to deeper, more productive shared thinking, the wrong kind of question can bring the process to a shuddering, jarring halt. Depending on the tone of voice, "How on earth did you get that conclusion?" may well invite me to tell you absolutely nothing more about my thinking processes. If you were to say instead "That's really interesting. I didn't think of it that way. How did you get to that conclusion?" the outcome could be very different.

Feeling Safe

The Habits of Mind discussed earlier are as important in the home as they are in the school. Parents can encourage their children to communicate with clarity and precision at home, around the dining table, in the car, and while watching TV. The familiar exchange of "What happened at school today?" followed by the response "Nothing much" is commonplace because the question was neither clear not precise. Schools can help parents understand that they will achieve much more if they ask their children instead to recount two good things that happened in class that day. They might like to make the question even more precise by specifying a particular class, a current project, or a liked teacher. Generic questions deserve generic replies. Remember that the techniques of questioning from Chapter 9 are just as valuable for the parents of the children in your class as they are for you. You can help parents think carefully about the questions they ask when they want to have a meaningful conversation with their child.

Communication is at the heart of helping children become skilled thinkers; it is encouraged when the experience is uplifting and affirming. We explore our thoughts by talking about them. Metacognition can only happen through the medium of language—how do I know what I think until I hear what I say? In metacognitive thinking, we are exposing and exploring our thoughts and turning them this way and that, trying to decide how well they were suited to the task, and how we might have made them better. We will only do this when we feel safe.

We enjoy doing things that make us feel good and are more inclined to do them. Feeling safe and feeling good about ourselves go hand in hand. Sometimes the things that make us feel bad and build up tension can demand our attention simply because we need to release that tension somehow. But tensions can be relieved in many ways, and a different kind of self-talk can help dispel negativity in a positive way that encourages the development of a more optimistic frame of mind.

The following example illustrates how changes in the way a parent asks questions can have profound effects. A six-year-old child was in her second year at school. After the initial gloss of a new school year and teacher had worn off, her parents became concerned because she told them that she had no one to play with at school and everyone was mean to her. They would ask her each day after school if things had been better that day, but nothing seemed to improve, and their talks about school always seemed to revolve around what was going wrong. She was beginning to resist going to school in the mornings and did not want to talk about her day when she came home. Communication about school was drying up. Eventually the mother approached the principal, who agreed to spend some time in the playground and report exactly what he saw. She was intrigued to get a phone call from him a few days later in which he told her that he saw her daughter playing happily with a group of children and they all seemed to be having a fine time. Clearly it was time for a rethink. It occurred to the parents that perhaps they were focusing on the bad things—and there will always be some of those in any day—to the exclusion of the good things because it caused them discomfort to think that their little girl was unhappy at school. They decided never again to ask "How was school today?" Instead, they would ask her to tell them a couple of really good things that happened that day—there are invariably some of those, too. Over the next few weeks, her attitude toward school began to change. As she paid more attention to the positive things, she began to enjoy school more, and her parents found they could talk about school again. Here we see the contagious nature of attitude. Opening up the doors to conversation about school provided fertile ground for thinking.

Let's Look at the Curriculum

Somewhere in the course of your education, you studied the history of the foundation of your country. You committed dates, names, and documents to memory. You might also have learned something of the periodic table in chemistry, how to conjugate the verb *to be* in French, and how to solve a quadratic equation. Where has all that learning gone? If you rustle around in the deeper recesses of your memory, could you discover it again, blow off the dust, and integrate it into your daily life?

As teachers, we all recognize that much of the factual knowledge we impart to our students will be forgotten after they have left our class. During the 1970s, the American comedian Don Norvello, in the persona of Father Guido Sarducci, performed a comedy routine called The Five Minute University based on this idea. His premise was that in 5 minutes he could impart all the knowledge that most university students remember five years after they leave school. Your Spanish language classes would be reduced to *¿Cómo está usted?* ("How are you?") and *Muy bien.* ("Very well.") Sometimes we can find deep truths in humor.

In our workshops with teachers, administrators, parents, and senior citizens, both in Australia and in the United States, we often ask, "What would you like students to remember five years after they have left school?" It is, perhaps, not surprising that the results are similar wherever we ask. Here are some of the most typical responses:

Recognize his or her abilities

Be creative

Be able to solve problems

Know what and how to study

Be self-motivated and confident

Be able to operate in a variety of environments

Recognize injustice

Be productive citizens

Be lifelong learners

Be able to work in teams

Be compassionate

Appreciate the value of education

Have a sense of humor

Have the ability to communicate clearly

Finish things

No one suggested that knowing the date of the Battle of Hastings was important. Nor was the ability to parse a sentence, conjugate French verbs, or solve quadratic equations mentioned. What was conspicuously absent was any reference to specific factual information.

The question we ask next is this: "Where do these real teaching objectives of parents, teachers, and administrators appear in the curriculum; where are they taught *with intention?*"

The notion of *intention* is important. If these are the most important, lasting outcomes of education, surely we need to do more than assume they will be caught indirectly by exposure to a positive school culture and by participating in the things that happen in our classrooms. Our curriculum statements, our planning documents, and our day-to-day lesson plans need to incorporate these behaviors and attitudes as specific learning outcomes. We need to have a wide repertoire of strategies that enables us to infuse these outcomes into all of our learning tasks. These long-range learning goals must be planned for and taught specifically, and should inform the way we go about teaching every discipline. In the Resources section of this book, you will find a suggested lesson planning template that explicitly incorporates specific thinking tools, behaviors, and metacognitive practices.

As we analyzed these responses, it became very clear to us that they reflected the behaviors of reflective, metacognitive learners and the dispositions of intelligent, successful people described by the Habits of Mind. These 16 dispositions provide teachers and students with a scaffold for metacognitive teaching. They provide us with the focus, structure, language, and strategies needed to teach *with intentionality* those things that ensure lifelong learning and productive participation in society after school. How do we ensure that the taught curriculum of a school will support, with intentionality, these fundamental outcomes of a successful education?

These shared values and attitudes will cut across subject and year-level boundaries. As schools grow larger, and especially in the high school environment, it is very easy for the teaching staff to become splintered. History teachers no longer talk with art teachers, and the mathematics department is seldom in conversation with the English department. Traditions are hard to overcome. Leadership within the school has the responsibility to ensure that there are both scheduled blocks of time and places for meetings of teachers from time to time that will facilitate these cross-boundary discussions. The agenda for such meetings should be designed to ensure that discussion does not revolve solely around housekeeping and organizational matters. Schools are complex collections of large numbers of people, and it is very easy for the smooth running of the organization to become the focus of meetings. Incorporating consideration of the role of thinking as an agenda item will ensure it doesn't get swamped by the deluge of procedural problems and issues. We talk about the things that are important to us, and the things that we talk about become the things we understand to be important. These discussions need to be explicit, focused, and purposeful; this is best achieved by working them into the fabric of organizational planning.

Parental Contributions to the Curriculum

School administrators and teachers can do a great deal to help parents understand both the importance of their child being able to think metacognitively and how much they can do to help in this development. Parents frequently ask how they can help; schools vary in their official responses to these requests. Too often parental involvement is interpreted to mean helping with homework. In some schools, parents are advised to stay right out of the homework issue and act only as a kind of marshal, ensuring that there is a place, a time, some peace and quiet, and, when the homework is finished, that it gets into the school bag ready for tomorrow. If the student gets stuck on a particular homework problem, some schools advise parents to simply inform the teacher the next morning in a note. In other schools, it is hoped that parents will intervene and act as a second line of teaching, working through the problem and guiding the student with additional explanations as needed. This approach can be difficult when parents discover that mathematics is taught differently from when they were at school, that high-school algebra is nothing more than a vague notion lurking somewhere in the recesses of their minds, and discussions on contentious issues from social studies rapidly turn into generational warfare.

There is a much more productive way for parents of students, from kindergarten to university, to help their children. It does not simply involve the policing of homework, nor does it require any understanding of the school curriculum.

The ability to think metacognitively—to think about their thinking, to recognize, monitor, evaluate, and adjust their thinking—is the foundation for successful learning in mathematics, history, geography, science, music, art, mountain climbing, cooking, bicycle building, or any activity that involves the human mind and problem solving. Parents do not need any knowledge of curriculum content to be able to help build this foundation, because metacognitive learning is active learning and it is *transferrable*. We as teachers can explore with parents our belief that thinking is at the root of all learning, and explain that we want them to help their children to learn how to be good thinkers. We also want them to help their children to talk and think about their own thinking—to be metacognitive. It is important to use the word *metacognition* regularly and to demystify it, because it really isn't a mysterious word, and the concept of thinking about your own thinking is not difficult once you start doing it. We just haven't been doing enough of it.

When parents ask how they can help their child in school, don't simply talk about homework. Instead, explain that they can help their child learn the most important skill they will ever need for successful learning at school and beyond—how to think. Even better, they can help their child become a metacognitive thinker who understands how his mind works and can choose the best ways to solve problems, evaluate whether or not his thinking strategies work, and learn from his experiences so that he does better next time. You can also explain that the miracle of this is that they can do it in the kitchen, in the car, or walking on the beach, and it need never have anything to do with algebra or long division.

Helping to Make Reading Time a Thinking Time

One of the central tasks of early education is the development of literacy. The inability to read fluently is a leaden weight around a child's neck.

Parents of young children are encouraged to listen to them read daily. What guidance do you give to parents to ensure that they emphasize the thinking part of reading and not just the decoding? Listening to a child read provides a rich opportunity to focus on the value of thoughtful responses as well as a chance to develop metacognition. When a child comes to an unfamiliar word, parents often feel that the appropriate reaction is to suggest sounding it out. This can be a very helpful strategy, but it should not be the first strategy. Instead, we should always ask the child "What would make sense?" When a child successfully works out what the word is, a metacognitive discussion can easily follow by asking "How did you work that out? What other strategies might have helped you work it out?" In this way, we reinforce the notion that reading is about making sense, that it is a thinking activity as well as a decoding activity. Too frequently, we approach reading as though it is fundamentally a code-breaking process, and this is no truer of reading than it is of learning to talk.

If we took more notice of the ways in which our children learned to speak in their infancy and applied that to how we help them develop as readers, we would have far fewer children struggling with literacy. Learning to talk was always about understanding each other and becoming a functioning, contributing member of the conversations that flow constantly around us. Imagine what would happen if we were to decide to instruct our babies in the act of talking and approached it as a decoding exercise—an approach that characterizes much reading instruction, particularly that based primarily on phonics. Babies want to understand the sounds and participate in the world around them; that meaning-focused intention is what propels them to master this extraordinarily complex task of language learning.

As educators, we need to inform parents of the need to keep the focus firmly on understanding and keep asking "What makes sense?" as the beginning reader struggles through the printed page, ensuring that reading both starts and continues as a thinking skill. The simple question "How did you work out what that word was?" encourages the child to think more explicitly about his strategies when faced with an unfamiliar word in a passage. He is thinking about his thinking—thinking metacognitively.

Check out the hints for parents that are listed in Reading as a Time for Thinking in the Resources section.

Thinking Through the Daily Routines

Daily tasks in the classroom and around the house can be made into opportunities to have a child thinking rather than simply doing. As parent and child share the task of emptying the dishwasher, they can talk about why various items are stored where they are. Parents can encourage thinking by asking if there might be a better place to keep the cereal bowls; if the child can give a good reason for changing things around a little, change them!

We sometimes complain about the number of *why* questions young children fire at us. Asking a child why she chose to do something the way she did can expose her thinking to reflection and the process of metacognition, but we need to keep in mind that the very young child's "Why?" can sometimes become irritating when we sense it is largely manipulative, as can the adolescent's "Why?" when it seems to be largely confrontational. Human beings seem to be very good at picking up ulterior motives and the unspoken messages sometimes hidden within questions. We can avoid a judgmental, confrontational, or inquisitorial tone when asking why a child or adolescent did something a particular way by framing our questions a little more carefully.

If we want others to reveal their thinking, we must make them feel safe. It is no surprise that aggressive, attack-dog style television interviewers end up with defensive politicians who reveal nothing, and hence we viewers learn little or nothing that is of value from them. There is no quicker way to shut down thinking than to make judgments. A positive evaluation of a particular line of thinking can discourage any further exploration, because the implication is that the thinker has already got it all "right." A negative comment about a line of thought pulls the ground out from under the thinker who is still exploring and trying out new ideas.

Let's imagine a situation where father and daughter are emptying the dishwasher together. Here is the conversation:

Daughter: Why do we always put the plates so far away from the dishwasher?

Dad: That's just where they always go. Do you think that's a bad place?

Daughter: I want to put them there (points to nearby cupboard)

Dad: We could do that. How would it help?

Daughter: Well, it's closer, so we wouldn't have to keep walking back and forwards to the other cupboard.

So they make room in the new cupboard and begin stacking the dishes.

Dad: How should we stack them?

Daughter: We could put the biggest things in first and then smaller things on top.

Dad: OK. (they stack plates, bowls, and saucers on top of each other)

Dad: How does that look?

Daughter: Well, it looks really nice, but we need the big plates more often than the saucers, and that means we will have to move the saucers every time we want a plate.

Dad: So what were you thinking about most when you decided how to stack them?

Daughter: I was just thinking about how they looked nice. I should have thought about what was practical too.

Dad: (laughing) Maybe we should have done that kind of thinking when we were arguing about what kind of car to get you!

Encourage parents to consider allowing their teenagers to rearrange their rooms, but explain the need for them to spend some time talking about why they want to put the things where they do. Encourage them to provide time for their children to think through their decisions. Even something as mundane as choosing where different clothes are placed in a closet or chest of drawers can become an opportunity for a child to think first and act later. Asking the question "What was going through your mind when you decided to put your socks and underwear together in the top drawer and your sweaters in the very bottom drawer?" is a metacognitive question because it is asking the child to examine his own thought processes, to think about his thinking.

Some negotiation of classroom rules can be the basis for metacognition as students question themselves about their reasons for judging one rule as just and another as unfair. Let your students develop their own guidelines for the distribution of play equipment for recess, or the ways in which particular classroom tasks, both desirable and onerous, are allocated. Time-out in some form is a popular means of responding to infringements of discipline and good order in the school. This time can be constructively used by requiring students to write or draw their thoughts about their motivations for acting as they did. This can then serve as the basis for a further conference at which these motives can be thought about more deeply and perhaps some alternative behavioral strategies can be developed together.

Trickle-Down Attitudes

It is easy to forget that the child who walks through the school doors first thing in the morning is the same child who has just dealt with home life issues and getting ready for the day. The child's attitude is a powerful force in successful learning, and our students arrive at school with deeply embedded attitudes that have developed throughout their lives as a result of interactions with parents and the communities both within and outside the school, as well as more transitory attitudes determined by the immediate events in their environment.

I recall the comments of an elementary school principal, new to her socially disadvantaged urban school, after watching the children emerge from the yellow buses in the morning air.

> They seemed so burdened. Their heads hung down, they were uncommunicative, and they appeared to be dragging the problems of the world to school with them. My first task had to be to do something about this. This was no way to start a day at school.

From that day forward, whenever she had the opportunity, she would be out the front of the school welcoming the fleet of buses as they rolled in. She would greet each student with a smile, a touch on the shoulder, a word of encouragement, and a question about their weekend. This principal understood the trickle-down effect of attitude. She knew these children were far from empty vessels when they arrived at school. If they were to learn, and to think about their learning—to become metacognitive learners—she needed to deal with their frames of mind.

Each member of the community helps to set the daily tone and temperature of the climate within the school, but perhaps none so clearly as the principal. An administrator who walks into the school in the morning with the burdens of home displayed on her face and a chip on her shoulder guarantees that the secretaries will catch her negative mood. As each teacher arrives in the morning and checks into the office, their moods for the day are edged in one direction or another by the reception and interactions they had with the office staff. Each teacher then carries that attitude into the classroom and passes it on to the students. This principal also described her "parking-lot strategy" for her own attitude management. Each morning she would park her car as far away from the front door of the school as she could. The walk from car to door was her adjustment time.

This trickle-down effect can be powerful; in addition, she knew how important it was to manage her attitude, and she spoke about this with the teachers at her school. Significant periods of coaching and professional development had given the teachers in her school a wider range of strategies for behavior management. As their sense of control grew, their attitudes to their students and to the task of teaching began to change. Gradually, the contagious nature of attitudes became crystal clear.

Sharing Thinking Strategies

As we have pointed out earlier, in order to be truly reflective about our thinking—to be truly metacognitive—one needs a language and a structure to think and talk about our own thinking. Members of a culture share a common language. The Habits of Mind provide a framework for discussing metacognition, and any list of cognitive skills such as Bloom's taxonomy or the thinking tools of Edward de Bono will provide a common language and shared meanings for discussing the type of thinking being used. When everyone uses a common language, a sense of coherence develops within the school community about what we believe is important and what we are striving to achieve.

Members of a community share the things that help their community thrive. As educators, we have created a wealth of resources and strategies that we use to encourage our students to be deeper thinkers; many are discussed in this book. Parents can make good use of these tools if only we make them available.

Thinking maps, for example, are a way of both exploring and networking, or linking, knowledge and are a common classroom tool. Let's share this one with parents and explain that as a family holiday time approaches, they can talk with their children about the options open to them and the limitations on those options, and then brainstorm about how to spend time within these constraints. Older children might benefit from the use of Plus, Minus, and Interesting (PMI) lists. Making a list of the things that they would love to do, the things they never want to have to do again, and the things that just look a bit interesting, provides focus for further thought.

A large sheet of chart paper on the dining room table, some colored pens, and some guidance about mind mapping is a great starting point, because mind maps are powerful metacognitive tools that enable us to expand on first thoughts, link ideas, and see connections. They are a means of deepening and broadening thoughts about any topic. If the family has a wall somewhere where the chart can be taped, family members can add ideas as they come to them, or simply leave it on the table for a few days and then come back to it for a discussion of a much more richly considered family holiday.

Mind maps are powerful because they are organic, dynamic entities. They grow into knowledge networks that mirror the way we believe our brains integrate information. Each one will grow and change as discussion and thought proceeds. The important thing is to keep digging more deeply and to keep looking for ways to link each new thought. Teachers understand the power of color and of nonlinguistic representations in learning, and so need to encourage parents to make sure their children use lots of color and include drawings and symbols when they feel it is appropriate. A child's simple drawing of a dog frolicking on a beach compared with a forlorn dog in a cage at a boarding kennel may help resolve a conflict between those two destinations. Adults, too, will benefit from drawing on both sides of the brain.

Planning the route for a holiday trip can also be a rich opportunity for metacognitive thinking. The parents give the map to the children and ask them to plot a route to their holiday destination. After they have finished their first attempt comes the time for assessment. "When you were working out the route, what helped you decide?" The children might say they were working on the shortest distance. "When you think about the trip, what other factors might be important in deciding the route?" Now the exploration begins to deepen, and suggestions of scenic spots, good eating places, and road quality come into play. By careful questioning and guidance, the parents can lead their children to think metacognitively and to understand that often our first thought is useful but misses a lot of important points, and so we need to reflect on first thoughts and look for options. When we find options, we may also find that they conflict with one another, so we may need to do some evaluation. In order to evaluate, we may need to do some research and get some more information. Taking the scenic route may mean a much longer journey, hence more gas, and it may pass through an area where there are very few gas stations. Route planning for the family holiday becomes an opportunity to think metacognitively, to identify the kinds of thinking, to monitor and assess their efficacy, and to modify or add to them if necessary.

Faculty meetings can easily become bogged down with an endless list of dot points itemizing pieces of information that could just as easily have been read. Meeting times are too precious in a crowded school schedule to waste them in this way. In a learning community, when people gather together professionally, they do so to learn, to think, and to get better at doing what it is they do. If a tool used in the classroom helps our students to think, it will also help *us* to think. It is not only children who benefit from the networking of their knowledge and from the use of nonlinguistic representation of their ideas.

Growing the Moral Compass

It may seem easier to expect children to simply do as we say because we are the adults and hence we have the authority. In the short term, it can save a lot of time. But if this is always our approach, what happens when we are no longer there to enforce the rules? If the child does the right thing because someone will punish her if she doesn't, how will she ever become self-sufficient? Where will her internal compass come from if we don't help her grow it? Staying clear of drugs because "I'll get hell if Dad finds out" is fine as long as Dad is likely to find out. Metacognitive thought around moral questions helps to develop young people who have an internal sense of morality. They have thought through issues and come to their own conclusions; just as metacognitive thinking enables them to recognize, monitor, assess, and adapt their thinking, it will help them to do the same with their behavior as they grow and become more and more independent.

An Incremental Process

Children do not become good thinkers overnight, after a specifically focused set of lessons at school, or after a "good talk" around the dinner table at home. Neither do the adults around them. It is an incremental process. Little by little, experience by experience, we become more adept at bringing the experiences of our daily lives within the sphere of our thinking minds. Parents can create a home environment where the time to think and talk about a problem is made available. They can also help their children to understand that it is equally important to think about our own thinking, to assess how well we are thinking, to have different strategies available to us, and to adjust and modify our thinking when we don't seem to be getting anywhere. When all participants are consciously striving to communicate with clarity and precision, to listen with empathy and understanding, to take in data from all sources, to seek humor when it can be found, and to gradually learn how to apply all 16 of the Habits of Mind to their daily lives, we know that they will become more effective problem solvers and learners, both at home and in society at large.

Summary

The ability to think metacognitively needs to be taught with intention and be reflected in our school documents. Developing a culture of thinking and metacognition in a school demands both explicitly shared values and supportive practices. School and home working together can achieve better outcomes for children. Parents often feel unqualified to deal with the curriculum content being covered at school, yet want to help their children succeed. We can help those parents understand the nature of metacognition and show them ways that they can help their students become more strategic thinkers who reflect on their own ideas. No knowledge of particular curriculum content is needed. We can help parents understand that developing a thoughtful child must be a priority. By finding the most appropriate times to talk and reflect, using routines around the house as opportunities for reflection, by planning together as a family, and by making best use of reading time with young children, parents can work with schools and lead their children to think about their thinking as part of every day's ordinary events. Schools can provide parents with both a time and place where they can discuss and learn about helpful metacognitive strategies that can be readily applied in both the school and the home.

THINKING DEEPER: DISCUSSION QUESTIONS

1. Imagine you are a parent walking into the front door of our school for the very first time. What would you see? What would you hear? What would you smell? What would you think? What do first impressions of our school say about the things we value?

2. What would an examination of our school's curriculum documents reveal to be our major intentional teaching objectives?

3. How closely aligned are our values and attitudes toward teaching with those held by the majority of our colleagues and our administrators?

4. Taking a clear and balanced look at our school right now, how involved are our parents in their children's education? What do we see them doing? What do we hear them saying?

5. What would we like them to be saying and doing?

6. How can the school best initiate an ongoing discussion with parents about the nature and importance of metacognition? How do we demystify the term?

7. What kinds of parental involvement does our current homework policy expect? Is this in line with what we now know about the role of metacognition in learning? How would a focus on metacognition empower parents in helping their children?

8. Can we provide a place where parents can meet, talk, and have a sense of ownership and involvement?

9. How does our school's discipline code encourage students to think about their behavior and develop a moral compass?

Resources for Teachers

1. Metacognition Monitor

2. Metacognitive Planning Template

3. Whole-School Assemblies

4. Reading as a Time for Thinking (Guidelines for Parents)

5. Parents as Partners in Metacognition: Planning Points for Schools

1. METACOGNITION MONITOR

What were you thinking about? (Content)	How successful was your thinking?
What thinking skills and tools did you use? (Cognition)	What would you do differently if you did this task again?
Which Habits of Mind supported your thinking? (Conduct)	

2. METACOGNITIVE PLANNING TEMPLATE

This is not intended to be a complete planning template. It is intended that it be infused into existing planning formats

Content
Level 3 science. Students will classify materials as solid, liquid, or gas.
Cognition: Thinking Skills
Identify, describe, name, list, compare/contrast, classify. Which ones can children already do? Which ones do I need to teach explicitly as part of this lesson? Do students know how to perform the thinking skills?   • Can students describe the steps in the thinking process?   • Can they correctly label the skills when they use them?   • Do they apply the skills spontaneously when solving problems?
Cognitive Tasks That Require Thinking Skills
Children will identify a series of pictures/drawings of materials and identify, describe, and name them.   • Teacher explains the differences between solids, liquids, and gases using three examples.   • Children work in groups to classify materials.   • Each group prepares a table classifying materials and adding any other materials they can think of.
Conduct: Activating Habits of Mind
The Habits of Mind focused on in this lesson will be Thinking Interdependently, Communicating With Accuracy and Precision, and Gathering Data With All the Senses.   Do any of these Habits need to be taught explicitly? If so, spend time examining, demonstrating, and role-playing the subskills.   • Each Habit will be written on the chalkboard and briefly discussed at start of lesson.   • One or two subskills for each Habit will be included.   • Examples of use will be acknowledged by teacher as children work.
Metacognitive Review
At the conclusion of the lesson, students will review the thinking skills and Habits of Mind that they used, either orally or using a Metacognitive Monitor. "How did you distinguish between the materials?" "How did you decide what they were?" "Could you have done it any other way?"

3. WHOLE-SCHOOL ASSEMBLIES

If there is a suitable venue within the school, regular whole-school assemblies can do a great deal to help develop a sense of community. Some schools may choose to hold them weekly, others less frequently. Whatever the timing, it is essential that they be seen as opportunities to share what is good about the school, to avoid using them as "housekeeping" opportunities, and to be as inclusive as possible.

- Keep in mind that these assemblies are about the school community, the school family. Have different times for special guest speakers, motivational sessions before testing, and the like.
- A regular schedule ensures that everyone knows when the next assembly will be so they can plan for it.
- Don't waste time—keep the program brisk and interesting.
- Give parents plenty of notice so they can organize their lives—list dates in the newsletter.
- Have a roving wireless microphone so that the person leading the assembly can move among the students and interact with them when appropriate.
- Welcome parents at the beginning of the assembly.
- Spend time working out an efficient, orderly way of getting all students into the assembly area and back to their classes. This should take as little time as possible.
- Have students arrive at the assembly empty-handed. That way there is less opportunity for distraction.
- Begin assemblies promptly and on time. Late classes will adjust their behavior when they discover that no one is going to wait for them.
- Encourage all teachers to participate in running the assembly.
- Spend a little time at the start of the assembly describing something positive that has happened recently.
- Have a Goal for the Week (or Month), and introduce it at the assembly; for example, "This month we are going to focus on managing impulsivity. Tell me three things you can do to help yourself with this." Write these three suggestions on a large whiteboard so everyone can see.
- At each assembly, assign one grade level to do a short presentation about work they have been doing.
- Have a Student of the Week (or Month) Award, and ensure that by the end of the year every student has been commended for something.
- Give special invitations to parents of students receiving awards.
- Select a Habit of Mind to focus on at each assembly. Have a group of students prepare and perform a role play demonstrating this Habit.
- Include time for some communal singing. Just one song can create a sense of fun and community when sung together.

(Continued)

(Continued)

- You will settle a large group of students much more quickly by commenting on the ones who are doing the right thing than by berating the ones who are not.
- Younger students respond well to echo rhythmic clapping, in which the teacher at the front claps a rhythm and everyone responds with an echo. This is another great way to settle them down and gain their attention.
- Games such as *Do as I say, don't do as I do* will also get students to focus their attention on the person leading the assembly.
- Invite parents who come to assemblies to share a cup of coffee with the principal afterwards.

4. READING AS A TIME FOR THINKING (GUIDELINES FOR PARENTS)

Fluent, confident readers are much more likely to become successful learners. Learning to read is intimately tied up with learning to think. You can make each reading session with your children an opportunity to help them develop metacognitively.

Here are some suggestions about how to make this happen:

- Read, read, read, read together. Every night. Close and snugly. Make sure your child can see the words. Talk about the pictures.
- When your child gets stuck on a word, the first question should always be "What would make sense?" Sounding it out is the way the child confirms which prediction was right.
- Encourage your child to follow along as you trace the words with your finger. Read the same favorites over and over again.
- Stop halfway through a sentence and let your child finish it. For example, if you read "The rabbit hopped into the . . ." and then wait, your child will chime in with the next word. Keep it happy, keep it fun.
- When you know the words your child is working on at school, help him point them out in the stories you read together.
- Help your child look for words that start or end with a certain letter in the stories you read together.
- Look for words with special endings—*ing, ed, er*. Look together for words with double letters—*oo, ee, pp*.
- Try and think together of words that rhyme with words you pick out from the story.
- When the book is familiar, encourage your child to read along with you. Slow down a little every now and then. At the easy parts, stop for a few words and let your child take over. It's a bit like letting go of the bicycle seat when you are teaching your child to ride a two-wheeler bike.
- Read all the print in your environment. Encourage your child to read street signs, cereal boxes, and advertisements.
- Write notes to your child. Put them in the lunch box, under the pillow, on the TV, or in her pocket.
- Write messages on the refrigerator door with a whiteboard marker. It will rub off.

5. PARENTS AS PARTNERS IN METACOGNITION: PLANNING POINTS FOR SCHOOLS

Below is a list of planning points that educators can use to help them design interactions between home and school that will encourage an understanding by parents of the role of metacognition in their children's lives at home and school. These suggestions can be used as a foundation for parent/teacher conferences, communication between school and home, and discussion groups involving educators and parents.

- Providing powerful homework help when you don't know the material: the difference between helping with curriculum content and helping with metacognition. The significant role parents can play.
- Fun thinking tools and strategies to use at home.
- Finding time at home to talk:
  - Meals together; the practical and the possible
  - Bedtimes
  - In the car
  - Weekends
  - Playing games together
  - Talking when the TV program is over

- The art of questioning for parents:
  - Questioning versus interrogating
  - Giving them time to think
  - Listening and making sure you understand, paraphrasing
  - Taking it the next step—probing
  - How not to be judgmental
- Incorporating metacognition in home/school communication:
  - a school slogan
    - "Metacognition matters"
    - "Sunnyhills, a thinking school"
  - posters around the school
  - a metacognitive, home-centered question at the head of each newsletter; for example, "How does your family plan for a holiday?" "What do your children think are the reasons for setting the table the way you do?" "What's your child's logic behind the way they put toys away (or don't put them away?)" "How do you deal with sibling rivalry?" Have you led your children to think about the reasons that lie behind the arguments?

- Agenda topics for meetings with parents:
  - The difference between remembering and understanding
  - Time Out as a time for thinking
  - The thinking behind phrases such as "Everyone has one"; "I hate vegetables"; "Nobody likes me"; "You never let me do anything"; "I'll do it later"

- The parents' role in projects. Helping the child predict the problems that might arise and developing strategies to deal with them. Creating a flow chart that sequences the tasks involved in the project and a checklist for noting completion.
- Encouraging thinking out loud—do puzzles together and talk about what is going on in your head as you work your way through the puzzle.
- The use of video games. Encourage your child to talk about the strategies used to succeed at a given level. What blocked your progress? What worked?
- Making predictions:
  - Bedtime conversations: "What was the best thing that happened today? What might happen tomorrow?"
  - Breakfast time conversations: "What are your plans for today? Are there any challenges likely? What is your plan to deal with them?"
  - Talking before sporting events: "How fast do you think you will run? What has changed since last time? What are some of your team's strengths?"

References

Adams, J., & Pendlebury, J. (2010). *Global research report: United States.* Leeds, UK: Thomson Reuters. Retrieved from http://researchanalytics.thomsonreuters.com/m/pdfs/globalresearchreport-usa.pdf.

Albert, R., & Barabási, A. L. (2001). Statistical mechanics of complex networks. *Review of Modern Physics, 74*(1), 47–97.

Anderson, J. (2010). *Succeeding with habits of mind.* Melbourne, Australia: Hawker Brownlow.

Anderson, L. W., & Krathwohl, D. R. *A taxonomy for learning, teaching, and assessing: A revision of Bloom's taxonomy of educational objectives.* New York: Longman.

Anzai, K., & Simon, H. A. (1979). The theory of learning by doing. *Psychological Review, 86,* 124–140.

Baggini, J., & Stangroom, J. (Eds.). (2004). *Great thinkers A–Z.* New York: Continuum.

Barabási, A.-L. (2002). *Linked: How everything is connected to everything else and what it means for business, science and everyday life.* New York: Plume (Penguin Group).

Barabási, A.-L., & Albert, R. (1999). Emergence of scaling in random networks. *Science, 286*(5439), 509–512.

Bernstein, B. (1971). *Class, codes and control* (Vol. 1). London: Routledge & Kegan Paul.

Bloom, B. S. (1956). *Taxonomy of educational objectives, handbook I: Cognitive domain.* New York: Longman.

Buoncristiani, A. M., & Buoncristiani, P. (2007). A network model of knowledge acquisition. Proceedings of the 13th International Conference on Thinking. Norrköping, Sweden. Retrieved from http://devisa-hb.se/thinkingconference/index13.html.

Butterfield, E. C., & Ferretti, R. P. (1987). Toward a theoretical integration of cognitive hypotheses about intellectual differences among children. In J. G. Borkowski & J. D. Day (Eds.), *Cognition in special children: Comparative approaches to retardation, learning disabilities, and giftedness* (pp. 195–233). Norwood, NJ: Ablex.

Chiabetta, E. L. A. (1976). A review of Piagetian studies relevant to science instruction at the secondary and college level. *Science Education, 60,* 253–261.

Costa, A. (2001). *Meditative environments in developing minds: A resource book for teaching thinking.* Alexandria, VA: Association for Supervision and Curriculum Development.

Costa, A. L., & Kallick, B. (Eds.). (2000). *Activating and engaging habits of mind.* 4 vols. Alexandria, VA: Association for Supervision and Curriculum Development.

Costa, A. L., & Kallick, B. (2008). *Learning and leading with habits of mind.* Alexandria, VA: Association for Supervision and Curriculum Development.

Damasio, A. R. (1999). How the brain creates the mind. *Scientific American, 281*(6), 112–117.

de Groot, A. D. (1965). *Thought and choice in chess.* The Hague, Netherlands: Mouton.

de Bono, E. (1968). *New think: The use of lateral thinking* (5th printing ed.). New York: Basic Books.

de Bono, E. (1970). *Lateral thinking: Creativity step by step.* New York: Harper & Row.

de Bono, E. (1976). *Teaching thinking.* New York: Penguin Books.

de Bono, E., (1994a). *Teach your child how to think.* New York: Penguin Books.

de Bono, E. (1994b). *Thinking course.* New York: Barnes & Noble.

Diderot. D., & D'Alembert, J. l. R. (Eds.). (1751/2011). *Encyclopédie, ou dictionnaire raisonné des sciences, des arts et des métiers, etc.* [Encyclopedia of the sciences, arts, and crafts, etc.] University of Chicago: ARTFL Encyclopédie Project, R. Morrissey (Ed.), Retrieved from http://encyclopedie.uchicago.edu/.

Dweck, C. S. (2008). *Mindset: The new psychology of success.* New York: Ballantine Books.

Ferguson, E. S. (1977). The mind's eye: Nonverbal thought. *Technology Science, 197*(4306), 827–836.

Feuerstein, R., Rand, Y., Hoffman, M. B., & Miller, R. (1980). *Instrumental enrichment: An intervention program for cognitive modifiability.* Baltimore: University Park Press.

Flavell, J. H., Friedrichs, A. G., & Hoyt, J. D. (1970). Developmental changes in memorization processes. *Cognitive Psychology, 1,* 324–340.

Friedman, T. L. (2005). *The world is flat: A brief history of the twenty-first century.* New York: Farrar, Strauss and Giroux.

Gonzales, P., Gúzman, J. C., Partelow, L., Pahlke, E., Jocelyn, L., Kastberg, D., et al. (2004). *Highlights from the Trends in International Mathematics and Science Study (TIMMS) 2003.* Washington, DC: National Center for Educational Statistics. Retrieved from http://nces.ed.gov/pubsearch/pubsinfo.asp?pubid=2005005.

Halliday, M. A. K. (2003). New ways of meaning: The challenge to applied linguistics. In M. A. K. Halliday, *On language and linguistics,* pp. 139–174. London: Continuum. (Originally published 1990 in *Journal of Applied Linguistics, 6,* pp. 7–36.)

Hamming, R. (1986, March). *You and your research.* Presentation at Bell Communications Research Colloquium Seminar. Retrieved from http://www.cs.virginia.edu/~robins/YouAndYourResearch.html.

Hatano, G., & Inagaki, K. (1986). Two courses of expertise. In H. Stevenson, H. Azuma, & K. Hakuta (Eds.), *Child development and education in Japan* (pp. 262–272). New York: Freeman.

Hoffer, E. (2006). *Reflections on the human condition.* Titusville, NJ: Hopewell Publications.

Jakab, P. L. (1990). *Visions of a flying machine: The Wright Brothers and the process of invention.* Washington, DC: Smithsonian Institution Press.

Jensen, E. (2006). *Enriching the brain: How to maximize every learner's potential.* San Francisco: Wiley & Sons.

Kahn, C. (2001). *Pythagoras and the Pythagoreans.* Cambridge, MA: Hackett.

Kelly, F. C. (1943). *The Wright brothers.* New York: Harcourt Brace.

Klein, J. (2008, March). *On the intelligence of crows* [video]. Retrieved from http://www.ted.com/talks/joshua_klein_on_the_intelligence_of_crows.html.

Marzano, R. J., Pickering. D. J., & Pollock, J. E. (2001). *Classroom instruction that works: Research-based strategies for increasing student achievement.* Alexandria, VA: Association for Supervision and Curriculum Development.

Merriam-Webster's Collegiate Dictionary (11th ed.). (2005). Springfield, MA: Merriam-Webster.

Moats, L. C. (2001). Overcoming the language gap: Invest generously in teacher professional development. *American Educator, 25*(5), 8–9.

National Academy of Sciences. (2006). *Who will do the science of the future?: A symposium on careers of women in science.* Washington, DC. National Academies Press. Retrieved from http://www.nap.edu/catalog/10008.html.

National Child Care Information and Technical Assistance Center. (2008). *State requirements for child-staff ratios and maximum group sizes for child care centers.* Retrieved from http://nccic.acf.hhs.gov/resource/state-requirements-child-staff-ratios-and-maximum-group-sizes-child-care-centers-2008.

National Research Council. (1999). *How people learn: Bridging research and practice.* Committee on Learning Research and Educational Practice. M. S. Donovan, J. D. Bransford, & J. W. Pelligrino (Eds.). Commission on Behavioral and Social Sciences and Education. Washington, DC: National Academy Press. Retrieved from http://www.nap.edu/openbook.php?record_id=9457.

National Research Council. (2000). *How people learn: Brain, mind, experience, and school.* Committee on Developments in the Science of Learning. J. D. Bransford, A. L. Brown, & R. R. Cocking (Eds.). Commission on Behavioral and Social Sciences and Education. Washington DC: National Academy Press. Retrieved from http://www.nap.edu/openbook.php?isbn=0309070368.

National Research Council. (2005). *How students learn: History, mathematics, and science in the classroom.* Commmittee on *How People Learn:* A Targeted Report for Teachers. M. S. Donovan & J. D. Bransford (Eds.). Division of Behavioral and Social Sciences and Education. Washington, DC: National Academies Press. Retrieved from http://www.nap.edu/catalog.php?record_id=10126.

National Research Council. (2006). *Rising above the gathering storm: Energizing and employing America for a brighter economic future.* Washington, DC: National Academies Press. Retrieved from http://www.nap.edu/catalog/11463.html.

Ogle, D. S. (1986). K-W-L group instructional strategy. In A. S. Palincsar, D. S. Ogle, B. F. Jones, & E. G. Carr (Eds.), *Teaching reading as thinking: Specific research-based strategies for teaching reading comprehension.* (Teleconference Resource Guide, pp. 11–17). Alexandria, VA: Association for Supervision and Curriculum Development.

Payne, R. (2003). *A framework for understanding poverty.* Highlands, TX: aha! Process.

Phillips, H. (2009). The five ages of the brain. *New Scientist, 2702,* 26–31.

Polya, G. (1945). *How to solve it.* Princeton, NJ: Princeton University Press.

Programme for International Student Assessment. (2003). *Learning for tomorrow's world: First results from PISA 2003.* Paris: Organisation For Economic Co-operation And Development. Retrieved from http://www.oecd.org/document/55/0,2340,en_32252351_32236173_33917303_1_1_1_1,00.html.

Ratey, J. J. (2001). *A user's guide to the brain: Perception, attention and the four theaters of the brain.* New York: Vintage Books.

Rockwell, G. (1999, January). *Diderot and hypertext.* Unpublished essay presented to the McMaster Association for Eighteenth-Century Studies. Retrieved from http://www.geoffreyrockwell.com/publications/Diderot.Hypertext.pdf.

Rowe, M. B. (1986). Wait time: Slowing down may be a way of speeding up. *Journal of Teacher Education, 37*(1), 43–50.

Russell, B. (1945). *A history of western philosophy.* New York: Simon and Schuster.

Schneider, W. (1985). *Developmental trends in the metamemory–memory behavior relationship: An integrative review.* In D. L. Forrest-Pressley, G. E. MacKinnon, & T. G. Waller (Eds.), *Metacognition, cognition, and human performance.* (Vol. 1, pp. 57–109). New York: Academic Press.

Sobulis, H. (2005). The philosophical foundations of the International Baccalaureate curriculum. *IB Research Notes, 5*(3), 2–7. Retrieved from http://www.ibo.org/programmes/research/publications/documents/notesoctober05.pdf.

Swartz, R. J. (2001). Infusing critical and creative thinking into content instruction. In A. L. Costa (Ed.), *Developing minds: A resource book for teaching thinking.* (3rd ed., pp. 266–274). Alexandria, VA: Association for Supervision and Curriculum Development.

Thomson Reuters. (n.d.). *Global research report series: United States.* Retrieved September 26, 2011, from http://researchanalytics.thomsonreuters.com/grr/.

Travers J., & Milgram S. (1969). An experimental study of the small world problem. *Sociometry, 32*(4), 425–443.

U. S. slide in world share continues as European Union, Asia Pacific advance. (2005). *Science Watch, 15*(5). Retrieved from http://www.sciencewatch.com/july-aug2005/index.html.

Vygotsky, L. S. (1986). *Thought and language* (Alex Kozulin, trans.). Cambridge, MA: MIT Press. (Original work published 1934.)

Walsh, J. A., & Sattes, E. D. (2005). *Quality questioning: Research-based practice to engage every learner.* Thousand Oaks, CA: Corwin.

Watts, D. J. (2003). *Six degrees: The science of a connected age.* New York: W. W. Norton.

Watts, D. J., & Strogatz, S. H. (1998). Collective dynamics of "small world" networks. *Nature, 393*(4), 440–442.

Weil, A., & Small, G. (2007). *The healthy brain kit workbook.* Boulder, CO: Sounds True.

Wells, G., & Claxton, G. (Eds.). (2002). *Learning for life in the 21st century: Sociocultural perspectives on the future of education.* Oxford, UK: Blackwell.

Wells, G. (2009). *The social context of language and literacy development.* Unpublished manuscript, University of California at Santa Cruz. Retrieved from http://people.ucsc.edu/~gwells/Files/Papers_Folder/documents/SocialContextofLandLDDraft.pdf.

Wheeler, R., & Swords, R. (2006). *Code-switching: Teaching Standard English in urban classrooms.* Urbana, IL: National Council of Teachers of English.

Whimbey, A. (1980). Students can learn to be better problem solvers. *Educational Leadership, 37*(7), 560–565.

Wiggins, G., & McTighe, J. (1998). *Understanding by design.* Alexandria, VA: Association for Supervision and Curriculum Development.

Index

CORWIN
A SAGE Company

The Corwin logo—a raven striding across an open book—represents the union of courage and learning. Corwin is committed to improving education for all learners by publishing books and other professional development resources for those serving the field of PreK–12 education. By providing practical, hands-on materials, Corwin continues to carry out the promise of its motto: **"Helping Educators Do Their Work Better."**